Literature and Belief

Literature and Belief

ENGLISH INSTITUTE ESSAYS · 1957

Edited with a Foreword by M. H. ABRAMS

1958 COLUMBIA UNIVERSITY PRESS, NEW YORK

21,984

OCT 23 '63.

Acknowledgments

"Belief and the Suspension of Disbelief," by M. H. Abrams, has appeared in the *University of Toronto Quarterly* (January, 1958), and "The Collaboration of Vision in the Poetic Act," by Nathan A. Scott, Jr., in *Cross Currents* (Spring, 1957) and in *The Christian Scholar* (December, 1957).

The quotation from *The Letters of W. B. Yeats* in the essay by Cleanth Brooks is used with the permission of The Macmillan Company. With the permission of Alfred A. Knopf, Louis Martz has quoted from the following volumes of Wallace Stevens's writings: *Collected Poems* (1954), *Opus Posthumous* (1957), and *The Necessary Angel* (1951).

Foreword

The first four essays in this book comprised the conference on "Literature and Belief" directed by Professor Cleanth Brooks at the meeting of the English Institute in 1957. To these have been added two essays bearing on the same topic—that by Professor Nathan A. Scott, Jr., from the conference on "Peripheries of Literature" in 1956, and that by Professor Louis Martz from the conference on "Wallace Stevens" in 1957.

In *The Critic's Notebook,* R. W. Stallman cites Allen Tate's judgment that the question of belief is today "the chief problem of poetic criticism" and apportions to the topic one-eighth of the pages in his anthology of contemporary *loci critici*. The equivalent concern of older critics had been with the apparent untruth of narrative "feigning," and the typical attempts to save the credit of poetry had been variants of Sidney's claim that the poet "nothing affirms, and therefore never lieth." Better to achieve his proper end of instruction, or pleasure, or both, the poet is privileged, as Father Bouhours put it in 1687, "to lie so ingeniously." In our time the locus of the discussion has shifted to the conditions of aesthetic experience in the reader, and the cause of our perplexity is no longer the occurrence of narrative statements contrary to historical fact, or even to empirical possibility, but the occurrence in the greatest poems of large-scale moral, philosophical, or religious assertions which seem to contradict assertions in other poems of equal aesthetic value, and which sometimes run counter to our own deepest convictions. We are apparently not puzzled any more about

> It is an ancient Mariner,
> And he stoppeth one of three,

but only about

> He prayeth best, who loveth best
> All things both great and small.

There is no longer debate about the relevance of belief to

> Nel mezzo del cammin di nostra vita
> mi ritrovai per una selva oscura,

but only about its relevance to

> In la sua volontade è nostra pace.

On this problem, after almost four decades of intensive debate, a broad critical consensus becomes apparent, once we disengage the aesthetic question from the theological and cultural questions which are often debated simultaneously with it. Most recent critics and aesthetic philosophers—including, I think, all the contributors to this volume—hold that, in appreciating literature as literature, the skilled reader in some fashion suspends his disbelief so as to go along in imagination with express judgments and doctrines from which he would ordinarily dissent. This is not the position that obtained in the days when Dr. Johnson, in his *Life of Gray,* laid down the principle that "we are affected only as we believe." The diversity of our literary heritage and, still more, the radical diversity in basic beliefs among the best modern writers, which have made the problem of belief a pressing one, have also enforced the theoretical tolerance of alien and conflicting beliefs. Whatever our individual commitments, we are all, as amateurs of literature, pluralists—under penalty of forfeiting our capacity to take delight both in the *De rerum* and *The Divine Comedy, The Wreck of the Deutschland* and *The Convergence of the Twain,* Eliot's *Ash Wednesday* and Stevens's *Sunday Morning,* Christina Rossetti's *Christmas Poem* and Yeats's *I saw a staring virgin stand, / Where holy Dionysus died.* So far we agree; disagreement begins with the secondary question whether the accident of sharing the beliefs asserted in one or another poem enters into the aesthetic experience proper, and if it does so, whether for better or for worse.

The viewpoint of critical liberalism is sometimes expressed in the extreme form: "No beliefs are relevant to aesthetic appreciation." But such an absolute predication, although given plausibility by its moiety of truth, is grossly undiscriminating. It exemplifies our tendency to posit a hypothetical poem, emptied of all particularity, and to assume that there is one question about the relevance of belief which is answerable by a single predication applying universally. There is no prior reason, however, why any statement about the role of belief should apply to all works of art, or even to all works of literature, which constitute, in Wittgenstein's terms, not a homogeneous class but a family of diverse individuals. Many current commonplaces about the aesthetic attitude, aesthetic distance, and the aesthetic object seem, in fact, to be grounded on a Cézanne still life, or an imagist poem, whose properties are incautiously extended to *King Lear* and *Paradise Lost*.

It is notable, and I think indicative of an important development in current criticism, that all the essays in this volume, however diverse their preoccupations and points of departure, converge on an area which is the meeting place for a reconsidered art for art's sake and a rehabilitated neohumanism. The common ground, express or implied, is that a work of literature is to be apprehended for its inherent and terminal values; but that, in so far as it represents human beings and human experiences, it involves assumptions and beliefs and sympathies with which a large measure of concurrence is indispensable for the reading of literature as literature and not another thing. The author of the first paper, in a survey ranging from lyric poems to allegorical narratives, finds that we must discriminate between overt assertions which we apprehend without consent, as purely histrionic moments, and built-in common sense and moral presuppositions from which, because they are essential to the work as a whole, we cannot withhold our consent without collapsing the poetic structure and draining it of its emotional power. Professor Bush points out that those works of Christian and pagan writers which, over the course of time, have worked their way to a high place on the literary scale share with each other, and presuppose in their readers, a central and essentially ethical humanity which transcends particular creeds. A religious poet, no less than a secular poet, is a great poet only in so far as he establishes a common base of human sympathies and values on which he can stand with his readers, whether they are believers or unbelievers. Unlike

the first two writers, Professor Brooks sets out from the claim
that a poem is an organic structure of partial meanings; yet he
finds that this verbal structure constitutes "a simulacrum of the
world of reality" and that it presents "a portion of the world of
experience as viewed and valued by a human being." As such it
requires for its success that author and readers possess "the same
set of general human responses" and share as criterion "the pattern of human nature that exists within us."

Father Ong reminds us that there is a voice behind the voices
in a literary work, and a person behind the dramatis personae.
Aristotle long ago pointed out that a speaker evinces a personal
character, an *ethos,* which itself functions as a mode of per-
suasion. Applying existentialist concepts, Father Ong shows how
complex is the process of literary communication, and that even
in nondidactic poetry our intimate sense of the author's presence
solicits our belief in him as a person who will either "say something worth our while or . . . betray our trust," as well as our
conviction, persisting even through dissent from particular details, "that something worthy of assent is being said, into which
the otherwise unacceptable detail may somehow be fitted." The
essay, it may be said, points to a neglected topic in recent criticism: the sense we get, even in the work of writers pursuing a
strict policy of authorial noninterference, of a pervasive *ethos,* of
an intelligence and moral sensibility (Henry James's "quality of
mind") which expresses itself less in manifest doctrine than in
the silent understructure of suppositions, norms, and beliefs
which have controlled the choice, conception, and management
of the literary subject. The role of such elements in the creative
process is precisely the topic of Professor Scott, who asserts that,

in its preoccupation with poetic autonomy and with the linguistic medium as very nearly "the enabling cause of a poem," contemporary criticism has "puppetized" the poet. It has lost sight of the essential ordering function not only of the poet's artistry, but also of the poet's "vision" of the world, constituted by "his most fundamental beliefs about what is radically significant," arrived at through all his experience as a human being, and exemplified not in the exposition of a thesis but "in rendering the human story." Professor Scott calls these constitutive beliefs the "religious dimension" of imaginative literature, but his is a spacious application of the term "religious" which includes what other contributors to this volume call the centrally human beliefs and values. And though he looks hopefully toward a day when the aesthetic and religious judgment of a work will coincide, he recognizes that in this fallen world the only workable requirement is not that of consent to the poet's doctrines, but that of consent to the poet's general view of life as "a *possible* view," such as might follow from an intelligent, sensitive, and sober consideration "of the facts of experience."

Finally Professor Martz directs our attention to the work of a major poet who set himself the explicit question "What, then, is the nature of poetry in a time of disbelief?" and who answered it by writing poems in which the meditative imagination is represented as imposing on the inhuman universe a human significance, order, and set of values, creating what it does not find. Here is a severe test case in poetic belief for the orthodox Christian reader posited by Professor Scott. For in what Stevens called the poet's "saintly exercises" he very cavalierly appropriated, as Professor Martz shows, the manner of proceeding in the meditative regimen practiced by the religious writers of the seventeenth century, but stripped it of all articles of belief in a divine being and a divine order and converted it into a purely secular and naturalistic enterprise—

> The poem of the mind in the act of finding
> What will suffice.

Stevens's poetry is the bold venture of a man in search of what will suffice, for whom the "human self," as he declared, seemed "all there was," leaving it "for him to resolve life and the world in his own terms"—that world (as an earlier meditative poet had said while he too still relied on the creative imagination in lieu of a Creator)

> which is the world
> Of all of us, the place in which, in the end,
> We find our happiness, or not at all.

M. H. ABRAMS

Ithaca, New York
January 6, 1958

Contents

Page vii Foreword
          by M. H. ABRAMS

      1   Belief and the Suspension of Disbelief
          by M. H. ABRAMS

     31   Tradition and Experience
          by DOUGLAS BUSH

     53   Implications of an Organic Theory of Poetry
          by CLEANTH BROOKS

     80   Voice as Summons for Belief
          by WALTER J. ONG, S.J.

    106   The Collaboration of Vision in the Poetic Act:
          The Religious Dimension
          by NATHAN A. SCOTT, JR.

139 Wallace Stevens: The World as Meditation
     by LOUIS L. MARTZ

167 A Selected Bibliography

173 Supervising Committee, The English Institute, 1957

174 The Program, 1957

177 Registrants, 1957

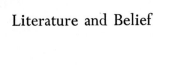

Literature and Belief

M. H. ABRAMS

Belief and the Suspension of Disbelief

Nominally the current preoccupation with the role of belief in literature goes back only some thirty-five years, to the issue as raised by I. A. Richards and debated by T. S. Eliot, Middleton Murry, and the many other critics and philosophers who took up the challenge. In fact, however, Richards's theory is a late stage in a perennial concern about the clash between what poets say and what their readers believe to be true. The problem of belief, in one or another formulation, is no less ancient than criticism, and it has always been argued in terms of "knowledge," "truth," and "reality," which are the cruxes of all philosophical disagreement. After twenty-five centuries, there seems greater weight than comfort in T. S. Eliot's weary conclusion that "the problem of belief is very complicated and probably quite insoluble." [1] But a review of the conditions of this endless debate may itself offer some possibility of headway. We have inherited from the past not only the problem, but the largely unvoiced aims and assumptions which control the way it

[1] *Selected Essays, 1917–1932* (London, 1932), p. 138.

is posed and answered, and to know how we got where we are may help us to decide where we are to go from here.

It all began, of course, with Plato. Plato's cosmos is the frame for the play of his dialectic, and cosmos and dialectic cooperate to force the consideration of poetry as a rival of philosophy for access to the true and the good, but under conditions—since poetry is an imitation of an imitation of the criterion Ideas—in which it is hopelessly out of the running. And how remarkably acquiescent the interlocutor in *The Republic* is to this management of the question! "Yes," "Quite true," "Just so," "That follows," "I agree." But suppose he had interjected: "Now look here, Socrates. I see your game. You've got me trapped in a set of premises by which the end is foreordained. But I refuse to consider poetry in a context in which it must aim to do what philosophy can do better. I propose instead that when we consider poetry, we consider it as poetry and not another thing."

Had the interlocutor delivered himself thus, the history of criticism might well have been radically different. It seems quite plain now that Aristotle's *Poetics* transferred the discussion to precisely these new grounds, but silently, so that over the centuries Aristotle has been interpreted as refuting or correcting Plato's theory on its own terms. As a consequence literary criticism has been maneuvered into a defensive stance from which it has never entirely recovered. Alone among the major disciplines the theory of literature has been mainly a branch of apologetics; and we shall mistake the emphases of many major critical documents, whether or not they are labeled a Defense of Poetry, if we fail to recognize the degree to which they have constituted the rebuttal in a persistent debate. The positions most strongly defended have shifted, to meet the threat from one or another enterprise claiming exclusive access to the kind of truth poetry was supposed to pretend to: philosophy, history, Christian theology and morals, and then, in the seventeenth century, the New Philosophy. But in every age the seemingly positive principles of criticism have been designed for the defense of poetry, and usually, as in the Platonic dialogues, on a terrain selected by the opposition.

Since the eighteenth century the situation has stabilized, for the great and portentous claimant to truth has become, and has remained, science. Consonantly, attempts to save the credit of poetry have been directed mainly against the pretensions to universal application of scientific standards of language, and against scientific criteria for judging the validity of all claims to knowledge and value. And quite early the pressure of a scientific culture gave their characteristic shape to two types of poetic theory which set the conditions under which we still for the most part undertake to deal with the problem of belief in literature. The first theory conceives poetry to be a special language whose function is to express and evoke feelings, and which is therefore immune from the criteria of valid reference, as well as from the claims on our belief, appropriate to the language of science. The second theory conceives a poem to be an autonomous world all its own, and therefore immune from the requirement that it correspond to our knowledge and beliefs about the world revealed by science.

Early in the nineteenth century Jeremy Bentham, heir to the traditional English semantics of scientific language, charged that by the standards of "logical truth" poetic statements are false.

"All poetry is misrepresentation." "Indeed, between poetry and truth there is a natural opposition: false morals, fictitious nature."[2] John Stuart Mill, a disciple of Bentham who became an ardent defender of poetry, although in terms controlled by the semantics of positivism, defined poetry as "the expression or uttering forth of feeling" and therefore what he called the "logical opposite" of "matter of fact or science." Accordingly, while science "addresses itself to belief" by "presenting a proposition to the understanding," poetry acts by "offering interesting objects of contemplation to the sensibilities"; so that the reader can accept it, without belief, for the sake of its emotional effects. Poetic illusion, he wrote, "consists in extracting from a conception known not to be true . . . the same benefit to the feelings which would be derived from it if it were a reality."[3]

By Matthew Arnold's time religion had become codefendant with poetry against the attack of positivism; and Arnold, accepting as inevitable the demise of dogmatic religion because it "has attached its emotion to the fact, and now the fact is failing it," transferred its function to poetry because (like Mill) he regarded it as emotively efficacious independently of its truth or the reader's belief. For "poetry attaches its emotion to the idea; the idea *is* the fact." And I. A. Richards, who used this pronouncement from "The Study of Poetry" as the epigraph to his *Science and Poetry,* expanded upon it in terms of a more developed form of the positivist semantics he shared with Hobbes,

[2] J. S. Mill, "Bentham," in *Early Essays by John Stuart Mill,* ed. by J. W. M. Gibbs (London, 1897), p. 208; Jeremy Bentham, *The Rationale of Reward,* in *Works,* ed. by John Bowring (Edinburgh, 1843), II, 253–54.

[3] *Early Essays,* pp. 202, 208; *Letters of John Stuart Mill,* ed. by H. S. R. Elliot (London, 1910), II, 358.

Bentham, and Mill. All language divides into two kinds. On the one side is "scientific statement," whose truth is ultimately a matter of correspondence "with the fact to which it points." On the other side is "emotive utterance," including poetry, which is composed of "pseudo-statements" whose function is not to assert truths but to organize our feelings and attitudes. And since we have learned to free the emotional efficacy of poetry from belief, poetry must take over the function of ordering our emotional life hitherto performed by the pseudo statements of religion.[4]

In our age, dominated by the odd assumption that all discourse which is not science must be of a single kind, many opponents of positivism fall in with the tendency to conflate religion with poetry in a common opposition to science. But this tactic will not do, whether we hold, with the positivists, that poetry will replace religion because it works without belief, or, with the anti-positivists, that poetry and religion share access to a special kind of nonscientific truth beyond logic and the law of excluded middle. On this distinguished panel I stand as an infidel *in partibus fidelium,* but I will venture the opinion that it is equally unjust to religion to poetize it and to poetry to sanctify it. Religion is patently not science, but no more is it poetry; and it can survive only if granted its own function and processes and claims upon belief. As for poetry, I shall soon maintain that it depends for its efficacy upon evoking a great number of beliefs. Besides, it must inevitably paralyze our responsiveness and ready delight to approach a poem as a way to salvation—in Richards's words, as "capable of saving us." [5]

To the view that poetry is an emotive use of language, the

[4] *Science and Poetry* (London, 1926), 56–61.   [5] *Ibid.,* p. 82.

most common alternative is the view that poetry is a world *sui generis,* to be experienced and valued on its own terms, independently of its correspondence to reality or of its emotive and moral effects on the reader. This concept also originated as a defensive tactic, this time against the demand that the materials of poetry be limited to the objects and possibilities of the empirical world revealed by the new science. In rebuttal eighteenth-century proponents of the mythical and marvelous in poetry developed the possibilities of the old Renaissance analogy—the most influential new concept in postclassical criticism—between the poet and the Creator. The poet, it was said, emulates God by creating a "second world" which is not an imitation of the real world, but a world of its own kind, subject only to its own laws, and exhibiting not the truth of correspondence, but only the truth of coherence, or purely internal consistency. "Poetic truth," as Richard Hurd said in 1762, is not the truth to "the known and experienced course of affairs in this world" demanded by Hobbes. For "the poet has a world of his own, where experience has less to do than consistent imagination." [6]

The radical implications of the concept of a poem as an *alter mundus* were exploited most fully in Germany, especially after Baumgarten for the first time set out to construct a philosophy of the fine arts in general, for which he coined the term "aesthetics." In Baumgarten's formulation, the end of a work of art is not to reflect reality, nor to foster morality or yield pleasure; "the aesthetic end is the perfection of sensuous cognition . . . that is, beauty." Produced by a poet who is "like a maker or a creator . . . the poem ought to be a sort of world," related to the real world "by analogy." Poetic fiction is "heterocosmic," consisting

[6] *Letters on Chivalry and Romance* (London, 1911), pp. 137–39.

of things possible in another world than the one we live in, and subject therefore not to the criterion of strict philosophic truth, but only to the criterion of "heterocosmic truth"; that is, self-consistency and the maximum internal coherence.[7] In his *Critique of Judgment* Kant added the corollary ideas that a beautiful work of art is experienced as an end in itself, by an act purely contemplative, disinterested, and free from any reference to desire, will, or the reality and utility of the object.

Now that these discoveries have become so commonplace that they seem the intuitions of common sense, it is easy to derogate the attempts of aesthetic philosophers to talk about all the arts at once. But the achievement of eighteenth-century aestheticians was immensely important: they made current a set of premises enabling the defenders of poetry to meet the charges of Plato and his successors, not on grounds that poetry can compete successfully with the philosopher, the scientist, and the moralist, but on grounds that poetry is entirely its own kind of thing, with its own laws, its own reason for being, and its particular mode of excellence. No wonder, then, that in the nineteenth century these ideas were enthusiastically seized upon and deployed (at first mainly on hearsay) by French and English theorists of art for art's sake in their strenuous counterattack against the demands for truth, morality, and utility in art by philosophical positivists, literary conservatives, and a society of Philistines. In his inaugural lecture at Oxford, "Poetry for Poetry's Sake," A. C. Bradley stripped this theory of its curious theological and ethical adjuncts about art as a religion and life as a work of art, and

[7] *Meditationes philosophicae* (1735), §§ 51–69; *Aesthetica* (1750, 1758), §§ 14, 441, 511–18, 585. See also Karl Philipp Moritz, *Ueber die bildende Nachahmung des Schönen* (1788).

gave it a classic statement. The experience of poetry, he says, "is an end in itself," and "its *poetic* value is this intrinsic worth alone." For the nature of poetry

> is to be not a part, nor yet a copy, of the real world . . . but to be a world by itself, independent, complete, autonomous; and to possess it fully you must enter that world, conform to its laws, and ignore for the time the beliefs, aims, and particular conditions which belong to you in the other world of reality.

And since this poetic world is an indissoluble unity of content and form, he decries in criticism "the heresy of the separable substance." [8]

For a lecture delivered more than a half-century ago, this sounds remarkably up-to-date. It should indeed, for its primary assumptions continue to be the grounds of the most familiar contemporary criticism. We assent heartily to Eliot's dictum that poetry is "autotelic" and to be considered "as poetry and not another thing." [9] We affirm with Ransom "the autonomy of the work itself as existing for its own sake," [10] and conceive the poem to be a self-sustaining entity—variously described as "an object in itself" or an "independent poetic structure" (Brooks) or an "icon" (Wimsatt) or "a kind of world or cosmos" (Austin Warren)—although, in accordance with the modern *furor semanticus,* we tend to think of the poetic other-world as a universe of discourse rather than a universe of creatures, setting, and events. And by a tactic reminiscent of A. C. Bradley's "heresy of the separable substance," and of "the heresy of the didactic" exposed by a still

---

[8] *Oxford Lectures On Poetry* (London, 1950), pp. 4–6, 17.

[9] *Selected Essays,* p. 30; *The Sacred Wood* (London, 1950), p. viii.

[10] *The World's Body* (New York, 1938), p. 343.

earlier proponent of art for art, Edgar Allan Poe, we severely pro-
scribe a variety of heresies and fallacies which threaten to violate
the independence and integrity of the sovereign poem.

This austere dedication to the poem *per se* has produced an un-
precedented and enlightening body of verbal explication. But it
threatens also to commit us to the concept of a poem as a language
game, or as a floating Laputa, insulated from life and essential
human concerns in a way that accords poorly with our experience in reading a great work of literature. Hence, I think, the
persistent struggle in recent criticism to save the autonomy of a
poem, yet to anchor it again to the world beyond itself and to
reengage it with the moral consciousness of the reader. One example is the frequent insistence that a poem is cognitive and
yields valid knowledge, although in the final analysis the knowledge a poem yields usually turns out to be coterminous with the
poem itself. The poem's value, as Allen Tate puts it, "is a cognitive one; it is sufficient that here, in the poem, we get knowledge
of a whole object." [11] By a procedure which has been a constant
corollary of the view that a poem is a world in itself ever since it
was expounded by Baumgarten and his contemporaries, the truth
of a poem is interpreted to be a truth of inner coherence, and the
relation of the poetic world to the real world is conceived to be
not a relation of correspondence, but of analogy. Just as A. C.
Bradley declared at the beginning of this century that poetry and
life "are parallel developments that nowhere meet . . . they are
analogues," so John Crowe Ransom's cognitive claim for poetry
comes down to the proposal that the structure and texture of a
poem are an analogical reminder that the world's body is "denser
and more refractory" than the "docile and virtuous" world repre-

[11] *On the Limits of Poetry* (New York, 1948), p. 48.

sented by poetry's great opposite, science.[12] And if I read him correctly, W. K. Wimsatt's point about literature as "a form of knowledge" is that poetic truth is inner coherence and the relation of a poem to the world is one of analogy. In his words, "the dimension of coherence is by various techniques of implication greatly enhanced and thus generates an extra dimension of correspondence to reality, the symbolic or analogical." [13]

We are particularly uneasy today about the pressure of the doctrine of poetic autonomy toward the conclusion of art for art; with a candor that is rare in contemporary discussion of this issue, Allen Tate affirms "that poetry finds its true usefulness in its perfect inutility." [14] The attempt to break out of the sealed verbal world of the poem-as-such is, I think, one cardinal motive for the current insistence that, in all poems which are more than trivially agreeable, the structure of symbols, images, and meanings is governed by a "theme." In practise this theme frequently turns out to be a moral or philosophical commonplace which bears a startling likeness to the "moral," or governing proposition, once postulated by the didactic theorists of the Renaissance and neoclassic ages. Homer, declared Dryden in his Preface to *Troilus and Cressida,* undertook to "insinuate into the people" the moral "that union preserves a commonwealth and discord de-

[12] Bradley, *Oxford Lectures,* p. 6; Ransom, *The New Criticism* (Norfolk, Conn., 1941), pp. 43, 281.

[13] *The Verbal Icon* (Lexington, Ky., 1954), p. 241. E. M. Forster wrote, in *Anonymity* (London, 1925), p. 14: In reading a poem, "we have entered a universe that only answers to its own laws, supports itself, internally coheres, and has a new standard of truth. Information is true if it is accurate. A poem is true if it hangs together." See also Philip Leon, "Aesthetic Knowledge," in *The Problems of Aesthetics,* ed. by Eliseo Vivas and Murray Krieger (New York, 1953).

[14] *On the Limits of Poetry,* p. 113.

stroys it; Sophocles, in his *Oedipus,* that no man is to be accounted happy before his death. 'Tis the moral that directs the whole action of a play to one center." The difference is that, according to the modern critic, the theme subsists only in the concrete embodiment of the poem, as an ownerless, unasserted, nonreferential, uncredited, and thoroughly insulated something which serves nevertheless to inform the meanings of a poem both with their unity and their moral "seriousness," "maturity," and "relevance." This existential oddity has been engendered by the opposing conditions of poetic autonomy and poetic relevance under which modern critics typically conduct their inquiry into the relations between poetry and life. As W. K. Wimsatt describes the conditions governing his essay on "Poetry and Morals": "We inquire . . . about the work so far as it can be considered by itself as a body of meaning. Neither the qualities of the author's mind nor the effects of a poem upon a reader's mind should be confused with the moral quality of the meaning expressed by the poem itself." [15]

I confess that my own view of the matter involves something like this divided premise, with its attendant difficulties. It seems to me that our experience in reading serious literature, when uninhibited by theoretical prepossessions, engages the whole mind, including the complex of common sense and moral beliefs and values deriving from our experience in this world. Yet I also think it essential to save the basic insight of aesthetic theory since the eighteenth century: that a poem is a self-sufficient whole which is to be read for its own sake, independently of the truths it may communicate or the moral and social effects it may exert,

[15] *Verbal Icon,* p. 87.

and that its intrinsic value constitutes its reason for existing as a poem and not as something else. I am also uncomfortably aware that this looks very much like an attempt to have art for art's sake and eat it too.

I would suggest that the apparent antinomy comes from relying too implicitly on aesthetic ideas inherited from a polemical past. The persistently defensive position of criticism, and its standard procedure of combating charges against poetry by asserting their contraries, has forced it into an either-or, all-or-none choice that breeds dilemmas: either language is scientific or it is purely emotive; either a poem corresponds to this world or it is a world entirely its own; either poetry has a moral aim or it is totally beyond judgment of good or evil; either all our beliefs are relevant to reading poetry, or all beliefs must be suspended. What we obviously need is the ability to make more distinctions and finer discriminations; and perhaps these will follow if we substitute for concepts developed mainly as polemical weapons a positive view designed specifically for poetic inquiry and analysis.

Suppose, then, that we set out from the observation that a poem is about people. Or a bit more elaborately, that a poem presents one or more persons recognizably like those in this world, but imposes its artistic differences by rendering the characters and their perceptions, thought, and actions so as to enhance their inherent interest and whatever effects the poem undertakes to achieve. This statement is not to be understood as contradicting the statements that a poem is an emotive use of language, or that a poem constitutes a verbal universe. It is offered merely as an alternative point of critical departure for inquiry into such questions as the role of belief in the appreciation of poetry. Furthermore, this viewpoint is as old as Aristotle's *Poetics,* and will produce no radical novelties. But I think the issue of morality and belief in poetry has been made to seem unnecessarily recondite because of the common tendency to define a poem as a special kind of language, or a special structure of words and meanings, and then to slip in characters and actions quietly through a back door.

I propose also not to begin with universal statements about "all poetry" or "all art," but to proceed inductively, beginning with single poetic passages and using these, in Wittgenstein's parlance, as "paradigm cases" on which to base only such generalizations as they promise to support. Convenient instances to hand are the few examples of poetic statements which have been mooted again and again in discussions of belief, although with little heed to their differences in kind and usually as illustrations for a foregone conclusion. The examples are: "Beauty is truth"; "Ripeness is all"; "In His will is our peace"; and "Thou best philosopher . . . Mighty Prophet! Seer blest!"

I

"Beauty is truth, truth beauty" is not asserted by Keats, either as a statement or as a pseudo statement. The Grecian Urn, after remaining obdurately mute under a hail of questions, unexpectedly gives voice to this proposition near the end of the poem. In discussions of the problem of belief the significance of this obvious fact is often overlooked or minimized. Middleton Murry, for example, although he observes that the speaker is the Urn, goes on immediately to reconstruct the biographical occasion Keats himself had for such a comment, and then (like so many other critics) evolves an elaborate aesthetico-ontological theory to demonstrate that the statement is philosophically valid, and merits assent.[16] For his part, I. A. Richards describes "Beauty is truth" as "the expression of a certain blend of feelings," and asks us to accept such emotive expressions without belief; and T. S. Eliot replies that he would be glad to do so, except that "the statement of Keats" seems to him so obtrusively meaningless that he finds the undertaking impossible.[17]

There is also a second and more important speaker in the poem. The whole of the *Ode on a Grecian Urn,* in fact, consists of the utterance of this unnamed character, whose situation and actions we follow as he attends first to the whole, then to the sculptured parts, and again to the whole of the Urn; and who expresses in the process not only his perceptions, but his thoughts and feelings, and thereby discovers to us a determinate temperament. By a standard poetic device we accept without disbelief, he attributes to the Urn a statement about beauty and truth which is actually a thought that the Urn evokes in him. How we are to take the statement, therefore, depends not only on its status as an utterance, in that place, by the particular Urn, but beyond that as the penultimate stage, dramatically rendered, in the meditation of the lyric speaker himself.

Obviously the earlier part of the *Ode* by no means gives the Urn a character that would warrant either its profundity or its reliability as a moral philosopher. In the mixed attitudes of the lyric speaker toward the Urn the playfulness and the pity, which are no less evident than the envy and the admiration, imply a position of superior understanding:

---

[16] "Beauty is Truth," *The Symposium,* I (1930), 466–501.

[17] Richards, *Practical Criticism* (1930), pp. 187, 278–79; Eliot, *Selected Essays,* p. 256.

Bold lover, never, never canst thou kiss,
Though winning near the goal—yet, do not grieve;
She cannot fade, though thou hast not thy bliss. . . .

The perfection represented on the Urn is the perdurability of the specious present, which escapes the "woe" of our mutable world only by surrendering any possibility of consummation and by trading grieving flesh for marble. The Urn, then, speaks from the limited perspective of a work of Grecian art; and it is from the larger viewpoint of this life, with its possibilities and its sorrows, that the lyric speaker has the last word, addressed to the figures on the Urn:

That is all
Ye know on earth, and all ye need to know.

The Urn has said, "Only the beautiful exists, and all that exists is beautiful"—but not, the speaker replies, in life, only in that sculptured Grecian world of noble simplicity where much that humanly matters is sacrificed for an enduring Now.[18]

I entirely agree, then, with Professor Brooks in his explication of the *Ode,* that "Beauty is truth" is not meant "to compete with . . . scientific and philosophical generalizations," but is to be considered as a speech "in character" and "dramatically appropriate" to the Urn. I am uneasy, however, about his final reference to "the world-view, or 'philosophy,' or 'truth' of the poem as a

[18] For another instance in which Keats uses "truth" as equivalent to "existence," see *The Letters of John Keats,* ed. by M. B. Forman (London, 1947), p. 67. I prefer attributing "That is all / Ye know on earth . . ." to the lyric speaker rather than to the Urn, because the former reading is at least as probable in the context and makes a richer poem. But even if we take the whole of the last two lines to be asserted by the Urn, the point holds that their significance is qualified by the nature imputed to the speaker.

whole." [19] For the poem as a whole is equally an utterance by a dramatically presented speaker, and none of its statements is proffered for our endorsement as a philosophical generalization of unlimited scope. They are all, therefore, to be apprehended as histrionic elements which are "in character" and "dramatically appropriate," for their inherent interest as stages in the evolution of an artistically ordered, hence all the more emotionally effective, experience of a credible human being.

Is an appreciation of the *Ode,* then, entirely independent of the reader's beliefs? Surely not. As it evolves, the poem makes constant call on a complex of beliefs which are the product of ordinary human experiences with life, people, love, mutability, age, and art. These subsist less in propositional form than in the form of unverbalized attitudes, propensities, sentiments, and dispositions; but they stand ready to precipitate into assertions the moment they are radically challenged, whether in the ordinary course of living or in that part of living we call reading poetry. Kant's claims, as I have said, seem valid, that the apprehension of a work of art, as opposed to our ordinary cognitive and practical concerns, is properly contemplative, disinterested, and free from will and desire, and that the function of presentative art is not to persuade us to beliefs or actions, but to be a terminal good. But here is where we need to make an essential discrimination. These observations are valid in so far as we are concerned to make a broad initial distinction between poetic and nonpoetic experience, and to separate specifically poetic values from effects outside the experience of the poem itself. But when applied to our apprehension of what goes on *inside* a poem, they seem to me, as

[19] *The Well Wrought Urn* (New York, 1947), pp. 141–42, 151–52.

often interpreted, to be not merely misleading, but directly contrary to aesthetic experience. If the poem works, our appreciation
of the matters it presents is not aloofly contemplative, but actively
engaged. We are not disinterested, but deeply concerned with the
characters and what they say and do, and we are interested in a
fashion that brings into play our entire moral economy and expresses itself continuously in attitudes of approval or disapproval,
sympathy or antipathy. And though the poet is not concerned to
persuade us to take up positions outside the poem, it is his constant concern to persuade us to concur with the common-sense
and moral positions presupposed by the poem, to take the serious
seriously and the comic comically, and to acquiesce in the prob-
ability of the thoughts, choices, and actions which are represented
to follow from a given character. All these results, however dis-
tinguishable from our responses in practical life, depend in great
part on beliefs and dispositions which we bring to the poem from
life; and these operate not as antagonists to our aesthetic responses,
but as the indispensable conditions for them, and therefore as
constitutive elements in our appreciation of the poem as a poem.
The skillful poet contrives which of our beliefs will be called into
play, to what degree, and with what emotional effect. Given a
truly impassive reader, all his beliefs suspended or anesthetized,
he would be as helpless, in his attempt to endow his work with
interest and power, as though he had to write for an audience
from Mars.

So with Keats's *Ode*. We accept without disbelief the given situation of the speaker confronting an Urn, and we attend delightedly
to the rich texture and music of his speech. But if what follows
is to be more than superficially effective, we must take the lyric

speaker's emotional problem seriously, as possessing dignity and importance according to the criteria of ordinary experience. By the same criteria, we must find the speaker himself credible and winning—sensitive, intelligent, warm, yet (unlike many of the profoundly solemn commentators on his utterance) able to meditate the woes of this life and the limitations of art with philosophic lucidity and a very lively sense of the irony of the human situation, and even of the humor of his dialogue with an Urn. Above all, we must so recognize ourselves and our lot in him as to consent imaginatively to his experience until it is resolved, in both artistic and human terms, in a way that is formally complete, hence beautiful, and intellectually and emotionally satisfying.

II

Whatever the case may be with the lyric, it had always seemed obvious that the words of a drama constitute speeches by determinate characters until several decades ago, when by a notable stratagem we critics succeeded in dehumanizing even Shakespeare's tragedies by converting them into patterns of thematic imagery. But I am bound by my critical premise to take "Ripeness is all" in the old-fashioned way, as a statement by a person in a given situation rather than as a moment in the dialectic of a vegetational symbol.

The statement is Edgar's, and it is not uttered in philosophical humor as a summary philosophy of life, but with sharp impatience, for an urgently practical purpose, at a desperate moment in the action. The battle has been lost, Lear and Cordelia captured, and Edgar must rally his blind father from a recurrence of his suicidal impulse, in the hopeless decision to bide and be captured:

EDGAR: Give me thy hand! Come on!
GLOUCESTER: No further, sir. A man may rot even here.
EDGAR: What, in ill thoughts again? Men must endure
    Their going hence, even as their coming hither;
    Ripeness is all. Come on.

The question of our giving or withholding assent to this statement, taken as a universal philosophic predication, has arisen only
because it has been pulled out of Shakespeare's context and put in
the artificial context of our own discusisons of the problem of belief. In its original place we respond to the speech, in the curt perfection of its phrasing, as following from Edgar's character, appropriate both to the bitter events preceding and to the exigency
of the moment, and also, it should be noted, as an element in the
action of people whose fortunes we strongly favor.

A popular opinion about Shakespeare's objectivity seems to
place his characters completely outside the purview of our moral
beliefs and judgments. It derives ultimately from Kant's concept
of disinterested aesthetic contemplation, came to England by way
of Coleridge and Hazlitt, and received its best-known formulation
in Keats's comment on Shakespeare's "negative capability" and
his claim that the poetical character "has as much delight in con-
ceiving an Iago as an Imogen. What shocks the virtuous philosopher delights the camelion poet," for whom all ends "in speculation." [20] Rightly understood, the concept is true and important.
We apprehend Shakespeare's villains with a purity and fullness
of appreciation possible only in art, where we see the characters
from within, and independently of the practical effects on us
of their being what they are. But the aesthetic attitude, though

[20] *Letters of Keats*, pp. 72, 227–28.

different from the practical attitude, is not so different as all that. In Dr. Johnson's phrase, the attitude is one of "tranquillity without indifference"; our aesthetic judgments, while not those of a participant, remain those of a partisan. We may take as great delight in Shakespeare's villain as in his hero, but we are constantly aware that the villain is a villain and the hero a hero. I. A. Richards has said in *Science and Poetry* that we must have no beliefs if we are to read *King Lear*. But *King Lear* presents a conflict of characters in which the author must make us take sides; and he is able to do so only by presupposing that we bring to the work deep-rooted moral beliefs and values which will cause us instinctively to attach our good will to some characters and ill will to others, and therefore to respond appropriately to their changing fortunes with hope and disappointment, delight and sadness, pity and terror.

Like all the greatest poets Shakespeare pays the human race the compliment of assuming that it is, in its central moral consciousness, sound. So from the opening words of the play we are invited to accept without disbelief the existence of King Lear and his three daughters, but to believe, and never for a moment to doubt—however the violence of circumstance may shake the assurance of this or that character in the play—that a king, while regal, ought to possess human understanding, moral penetration, and a modicum of humility, and that daughters should be loyal, kindly, and truthful, not treacherous, sadistic, and murderous. Shakespeare does not lay out Dante's geometrical distinctions between the utterly damnable and the merely damnable, but he does presuppose that we find good to be admirable and evil abhorrent, in the nuance of their manifestations in concrete behavior. We relish a villain like Edmund, skillfully rendered by the poet in all his unillusioned intelligence, self-insight, and vitality. But if, through some lapse in the author or some obtuseness or obliquity in ourselves, we remain indifferent, paring our fingernails, or so lose our moral bearings as to attach our sympathies to Edmund and the pelican daughters instead of to Lear and Gloucester (however flawed) and to Cordelia, Edgar, and Kent, then the play collapses into an amorphous mass without catastrophe or catharsis.

III

Far from Dante himself asserting that "In His will is our peace," he portrays Piccarda making the assertion to him, in smiling commiseration for the narrowness and pettiness of his earthly mind, and in a tone as near reproof as is possible for a spirit in felicity. For Dante has just inquired whether Piccarda is not dissatisfied with her place on the lowest of the heavenly spheres, and she replies that God draws all wills to what he wills, so that "In His will is our peace; it is that sea to which all moves." And Dante is enlightened and convinced: "Clear was it then to me how every where in heaven is Paradise."

This statement, then, like our earlier examples, is uttered in a dramatic context. There are, however, important differences in its literary conditions. The poem is not lyric or dramatic, but narrative in form; the author himself plays a role both as narrator and as one of his own characters; the total assertion this time involves a theological sub-proposition ("God exists"); and the passage occurs in a work of which the aim is not presentative, but didactic.

So Dante himself insists in his *Letter to Can Grande*. His work, he says there, is allegorical; its purpose "is to remove those living in this life" from misery to happiness; and its genus is ethical, "for the whole and the part are devised not for the sake of speculation but of possible action" (§§ 7-16). The *Divine Comedy,* then, like *Paradise Lost, Prometheus Unbound, A Doll's House,* and *Lady Chatterley's Lover,* is a work of literature specifically designed to dramatize and empower a set of beliefs. In it Piccarda's statement about God's will (in Dante's words) is one of the many things "that have great utility and delight" which are asked from the blessed souls in heaven "who see all the truth" (§ 33). The function of this statement is not, like that of "Ripeness is all," merely to instance character and advance the action, but to render in a dramatic, and therefore in the most efficacious possible way—as a truth achieved through error—a universal doctrine which is one aspect of the total theological truth propagated by the poem. For the first time in our discussion, accordingly, it becomes relevant to consider the relation of the reader's beliefs to his apprehension of an isolated poetic statement, offered for his assent. And the testimony of innumerable readers demonstrates that the passage can certainly be appreciated, and appreciated profoundly, independently of assent to its propositional truth. It touches sufficiently on universal experience—since all of us, whether Catholic, Protestant, or agnostic, know the heavy burden of individual decision—to enable us all to realize in imagination the relief that might come from saying to an infallible Providence, "Not my will, but Thine be done." This ability to take an assertion hypothetically, as a ground for imaginative experience, is one we in fact possess, and the business of critical theory is to recognize and confirm our reading skills, not to in-hibit them by arguments from inadequate premises.

The *Divine Comedy,* however, raises other questions about the role of belief which are specific to thesis narratives. What Dante undertakes, as a poet, is so to realize his abstract theological scheme as to transform our intellectual assent, which he largely takes for granted, into emotional consent and practical action. This task sets him extraordinarily difficult artistic problems. To take one striking example, he must persuade us, against all our natural inclinations, that the Inferno, with its savage, repulsive, and exquisitely ingenious tortures protracted in perpetuity, is not only required by God's justice but (as the Gate of Hell an-nounces) is entailed by God's "Primal Love." And the more credible and terrifying Dante, in his one function as moral moni-tor, makes the exemplary sufferings of the damned, the more difficult he makes his other task of winning our emotional con-sent to the thesis that God is Love, and Hell follows.

To this end Dante inserts himself, a mortal like us, into the poem as the experiential center through whose eyes and sensi-bility we invariably view Hell, as well as Purgatory and Heaven. And he exhibits with entire credibility the terror, the anguish, the incomprehension, the divided mind and emotions of the finite and temporal intelligence which is forced to look upon the universe under the aspect of eternity. He repeatedly misap-plies his sympathy, feels an irrepressible admiration for the strength and dignity of some of the sinners in their ultimate adversity, weeps with such an abandon of fellow-feeling that Virgil must sternly reprimand him, and when he hears Fran-cesca's tender story, faints with pity.

Dante's invention of himself is the supreme artistic achievement of the *Divine Comedy*. For Dante is a poet, though a didactic poet, and like any poet must endow his work with emotional power by engaging the sympathies and feelings of his readers with the matters he presents. To do so he appeals not merely to our theological beliefs (which we can yield or deny him) but also to beliefs and attitudes which are broader than any particular creed, and almost irresistibly compelling; for all of us, whatever our doctrinal differences, share the humanity of his central character and so follow and consent to his entirely human experiences, whether of the inhuman horrors of the doomed in Hell or the inhuman felicity of the Saints in Heaven.

Since he is, however, though a poet, a didactic poet, Dante relies on our prior beliefs and sentiments to involve us with the matters he shows forth, not as an end in itself, but as a means toward retroacting upon and reforming our beliefs and sentiments. If we circumvent him by stopping at the appreciation of what he shows forth, he would no doubt consider his great undertaking a failure. But for most of us the enjoyment of his didactic poem as, simply, a poem must perforce be enough.

IV

In our final example the question of belief is raised by the author himself, and in a form that makes it especially pertinent to contemporary literature. Wordsworth told Isabella Fenwick in 1843 that his *Ode: Intimations of Immortality* was based on experiences of his own childhood which he regarded "in the poem . . . as presumptive evidence of a prior state of existence." But he did not, he affirms, mean "to inculcate such a belief." "I took hold of the notion of preexistence as having sufficient foundation in humanity for authorizing me to make for my purpose the best use of it I could as a poet." [21]

With Wordsworth we impinge on our own age of self-consciousness about multiple choices in beliefs when, as T. S. Eliot declared, it is impossible to say how far some poets "write their poetry because of what they believe, and how far they believe a thing merely because they see that they can make poetry out of it." [22] William Blake had already created his own mythical system lest he "be enslaved by another man's," and thereby set the example for the spirits who came to give Yeats "metaphors for poetry." [23] So Wordsworth tells us that he did not mean to assert Platonic metempsychosis, but utilized it as an available poetic premise, an as-if ground for a metaphorical structure by which to manage what he called "the world of his own mind."

In this comment Wordsworth probably remembered what Coleridge had said about the *Ode* in the *Biographia Literaria* some twenty-six years earlier. There Coleridge described poetic illusion as "that *negative* faith, which simply permits the images presented to work by their own force, without either denial or affirmation of their real existence by the judgment." In the same chapter he went on to justify Wordsworth's use of Platonic preexistence as an uncredited poetic postulate, necessary in order to deal with "modes of inmost being, to which . . . the attributes of time and space are inapplicable and alien, but which yet can

---

[21] *The Poetical Works of William Wordsworth*, ed. by E. de Selincourt (Oxford, 1940–49), IV, 463–64.

[22] "Poetry and Propaganda," in *Literary Opinion in America*, ed. by Morton Dauwen Zabel (New York, 1951), p. 103.

[23] Blake, *Jerusalem*, 1.10; Yeats, *A Vision* (New York, 1938), p. 8.

not be conveyed save in symbols of time and space." But Coleridge refused equal immunity from disbelief to those lines in the *Ode* hailing a six-year-old child as "Thou best philosopher . . . Mighty Prophet! Seer blest!" "In what sense," he demands, "can the magnificent attributes . . . be appropriated to a child, which would not make them equally suitable to a bee, or a dog, or a field of corn?" For "the child is equally unconscious of it as they."[24]

In his *Coleridge on Imagination,* I. A. Richards took Coleridge severely to task for this limitation on the principle of suspended disbelief. For "we may," he said, "if we wish, take all the alleged attributes of Wordsworth's child," and even their applicability to a field of corn, "as fictions, as part of the myth."[25] But again, I think, we need to make distinctions. While it is true that the poet may educe from the myth of preexistence the conclusion that a child is the best philosopher, the myth by no means enforces this conclusion, as Plato's original use of it amply demonstrates. We must remember that Wordsworth's *Ode,* as he himself said, is not primarily about the myth; rather, the myth is auxiliary to the poetic management of events in this life to which every one, "if he would look back, could bear testimony." The lyric, we can say, presents the meditation of a man like ourselves, confronted abruptly by the need to adapt himself to a discovery which, in one or another form, is universally human: the discovery that in losing his youth he has lost the possibility of experiences on which he places the highest value. The postulate

---

[24] *Biographia Literaria,* ed. by J. Shawcross (Oxford, 1907), II, 107, 111–13, 120–21.
[25] *Coleridge On Imagination* (London, 1934), pp. 135–37.

of the preexistence of the soul, realized in the great image of the rising and westering sun, affords him the spatial and temporal metaphors he needs in order to objectify, dignify, and resolve what Coleridge called "a fact of mind." Ultimately the resolution depends on a shift in the point of view. From the vantage of the "imperial palace" of our origin, the earth is a "prison-house" and the process of aging a cumulative loss. But from the alternate vantage of this earth and this life—with its acquisitions of strength, sympathy, faith, and the philosophic mind, which spring from the very experience of human suffering—maturity is seen to have compensatory rewards; so that the metaphoric sun of the initial myth, which has risen "trailing clouds of glory," sets as the material sun we know in this world, yet takes another, if more sober, coloring from an eye "That hath kept watch o'er man's mortality."

What Coleridge queries is the credibility, in a poem which bears on our ordinary experience, and after Wordsworth has already described a very realistic six-year-old at his childish games, of the sudden apostrophe:

> Thou best Philosopher, who yet dost keep
> Thy heritage, thou Eye among the blind,
> That, deaf and silent, read'st the eternal deep,

.   .   .   .

> Mighty Prophet! Seer blest!

This is grandly said, but I understand and think I share Coleridge's sensation that, in its place and circumstances, it arouses counterbeliefs about real urchins which enforce an impression of what Coleridge called "mental bombast." If a child is a philosopher only in the sense that a field of corn is one, why the passionate and superlative encomium?

But this is a delicate decision, and I would not insist on it against contrary judgments by Richards, Brooks, and other expert readers. I want to insist, however, on the validity of Coleridge's implicit principle. A poet is entitled to his initial predication, or myth, or donnée, whether or not he is prepared to assert it outside the poem, and especially if, as Wordsworth said, it has "sufficient foundation in humanity" for his purpose "as a poet." But the inference is not justified that, from then on, anything goes. The poet must still win our imaginative consent to the aspects of human experience he presents, and to do so he cannot evade his responsibility to the beliefs and prepossessions of our common experience, common sense, and common moral consciousness. Even a phantasy such as the *Ancient Mariner,* Coleridge noted, requires a protagonist endowed with "a human interest and a semblance of truth sufficient to procure . . . that willing suspension of disbelief for the moment, which constitutes poetic faith"; [26] and in a more recent literary nightmare, Kafka put at the center of *The Trial* the matter-of-fact character K., to whose extraordinary experiences we acquiesce because his responses are so entirely ordinary.

The artistic cost of failure in this essential respect is demonstrated by the writings of accomplished craftsmen in which the substance is too inadequately human to engage our continuing interest, or which require our consent to positions so illiberal, or eccentric, or perverse that they incite counterbeliefs which in-

[26] *Biographia Literaria,* II, 6.

hibit the ungrudging "yes" that we grant to masterpieces. Blake's prophetic poems, for instance, lack what the *Divine Comedy* possesses—a human center of reference on which the imagination can rest; so that, fine isolated passages apart, and when we have exhausted their interest as symbolic puzzles, they become not a little tedious. Swinburne solicits our sympathy for modes of feeling so *outré* that a number of his lyrics remain brilliant items of literary *curiosa,* teetering on the edge of self-parody. In *The Counterfeiters* André Gide lavishes his intricate art to beguile us into taking seriously a resolution in which a nephew cohabits with his uncle, but the inherent risibility of an anomaly which is multiplied so ingeniously makes the resolution precarious. The difficulty is not in the literary material as such. Vladimir Nabokov's recent *Lolita,* which treats a somewhat parallel and even more scabrous matter, seems to me humanly right in inviting an attitude of horrified hilarity toward Humbert Humbert, on whom outrageous nature has forced the grotesque role of parent and paramour to a bobby-soxer. Ernest Hemingway's *The Short Happy Life of Francis Macomber* is a triumph of spare artistry. The discovery, however, that all depends on the street-corner assumption that a man's physical courage, his sexual virility, and his dominance over his wife are mutually implicative, provokes a skepticism which makes the triumph a somewhat hollow one. We have been assured that D. H. Lawrence is one of the few English novelists in the Great Tradition; yet, for all the power of the individual scenes, perhaps other readers share my imperfect accord with many of his protagonists: the Aaron of *Aaron's Rod,* for example, who deserts his wife and children to give unfettered scope to his ego, only to end by delivering his will over to the writer Lilly, that peculiarly Laurentian version of the God-given Great Man.

Here we reach the twilight zone between reasoned discussion of a critical problem and the expression of idiosyncrasy, and it is important not to let disagreement about particular applications obscure the issue in question. The implicit but constant requisition of a serious literary work upon our predispositions and beliefs is not an end in itself, but a necessary means to engage our interest and feelings, in order to move them toward a resolution. Furthermore, the great writer does not merely play upon the beliefs and propensities we bring to literature from life, but sensitizes, enlarges, and even transforms them. But in order to get sufficient purchase on our moral sensibility to accommodate it to the matters he presents, any writer must first take that sensibility as he finds it. There is no escaping the circumstance that a poet must submit to the conditions of human nature in order to be their master.

Tradition and Experience

The problem of poetry and belief, if not quite so old as poetry itself, is at least as old as philosophy. We remember Plato's account of the efforts of mythographers to explain away, by means of allegory, the indecorous behavior of Homer's gods. The same kind of problem arose early in the Christian era: miracles in both the Old and the New Testament were expounded by some of the church fathers as allegorical, not literal—to the great relief of the young and troubled Augustine. For Christians confronted with pagan literature the well-tried allegorical defense was again invoked, and throughout the Middle Ages allegorical interpretation was carried on. Not only the *Aeneid* but even Ovid's *Metamorphoses* was revamped in moral and religious terms. Such interpretations did not of course preclude aesthetic enjoyment. Then there were general handbooks of mythology composed on the same principle; the most famous of the earlier ones was the product of Boccaccio's sober years. Later and more learned handbooks of this kind were written up into the seventeenth century and were used by such poets as Spenser and Chapman and Jonson, as poets of our time have used *The*

Golden Bough. The allegorical interpretation of myth went along with a conscious effort to see this body of fable as a corrupted version of biblical truth; the flood described by Ovid was clearly a pagan story of Noah's flood, and so on.

It might be said that in our time the traditional problem has been reversed. Whereas the Middle Ages and the Renaissance were concerned with making pagan literature not only safe but morally helpful for Christian readers, the problem now is to make Christian literature acceptable to predominantly pagan readers in what it has become fashionable to call the post-Christian era. To put the case in that way is doubtless to exaggerate, and some qualifications will be made as we go on. To make a large one now, the problem of poetry and belief takes in far more than religious creeds. Two great poets of our age exemplify opposite poles: while the middle and later Eliot poses the religious problem with full immediacy, the reading of Yeats does not require belief in his fantastic "system." But Yeats is a special illustration of a larger modern problem: a poet of religious temperament, he had been cut off by science from Christianity and felt obliged to construct an imaginative world of symbols in which he could feel at home. In an age dominated by science and scientific method, some people ask if poetry, which is born of individual intuition, can claim any validity at all. In such an age, when scientific truth is commonly regarded as the only kind of truth, Coleridge's classic phrase, "that willing suspension of disbelief for the moment which constitutes poetic faith," may not seem a very positive validation for poetry. I. A. Richards, certainly a friend of poetry—and one who has lately turned poet himself—perhaps betrayed something of our age's scientific bias when he tried to establish poetry on solid ground by calling it pseudo statement, as distinguished from the statements of science.

However, the problem as a whole is much too complicated for one discussion, at least by me, and I should like to concentrate on one question: how far can the non-Christian reader apprehend and assimilate poetry more or less based on Christian belief, and belief of an older and more fundamentalist kind than that of modern liberal Protestantism? This limited but still large question has been much in the air during the last twenty-five years or so, especially because of Mr. Richards's formulations and Mr. Eliot's remarks on the modern reader's approach to Dante. Since I myself do not breathe easily in the rarefied air of aesthetic theory, I should like to pretend that all this modern discussion does not exist and offer, as it were, a first report from the literary equivalent of the man in the street—or perhaps I should say the man in the classroom.

Before we settle down with particular poets, a few more generalities may be allowed. It may be assumed that Christian readers, Catholic or Protestant, have no serious difficulties with either the writings of Catholics or the literature of traditional Protestantism. In many years of teaching Milton, I cannot recall that Catholic students, including priests and nuns, ever had trouble with *Paradise Lost;* and Sister Miriam Joseph has lately written a monograph on the Catholicity of what people have been so much given to calling the Puritan epic.

Some problems do arise for Christian readers of non-Christian literature, which is a large part of the world's writing in prose and verse. Christians of critical sophistication, who are presumably not very numerous, may study and aesthetically enjoy much that they regard as inadequate or erroneous. For Cardinal Newman the study of literature was a plain necessity for people living in the world, but it was also a matter of regret that the mass of the world's literature is "the Life and Remains of the *natural* man," "the science or history, partly and at best of the natural man, partly of man fallen": "I say, from the nature of the case, if Literature is to be made a study of human nature, you cannot have a Christian literature. It is a contradiction in terms to attempt a sinless Literature of sinful man." One may wonder what Newman would have thought of Graham Greene or Mauriac.

No modern reader is likely to apply more rigorously Christian criteria than Professor Hoxie N. Fairchild, whose fourth volume came out this year, and he has found very little English poetry between 1700 and 1880 that is both Christian and poetry, though his active aesthetic sensibility has not been starved. Mr. Fairchild's definition of a religious person—one admittedly inadequate for a Christian—posits belief in the insufficiency of man and the transcendent objectivity of God. Most of us are likely to accept that definition, even if we tend to use it less strictly than he does; and perhaps we might wish to include under religion, as no doubt Mr. Fairchild would, a concern for righteousness and for love. Mr. Fairchild's latest volume covers that special and conspicuous category of poems, from Tennyson, Browning, Arnold, and others, which grapple directly with the Victorian problem of faith and which most people, whatever their degree of doctrinal or aesthetic approval, would call religious, though Mr. Fairchild would not. He avowedly likes the poetry of real belief or real disbelief and dislikes what he considers the idealistic smudges, emotional and verbal, of those poets who grope in twilight; he prefers *The City of Dreadful Night* to *The Dream of Gerontius*—and *The Dream of Gerontius* to *Merlin and the Gleam*. He has much less sympathy with *In Memoriam* than Mr. Eliot has.

We are left with, or return to, the non-Christian reader's reactions to literature in the Christian tradition, though some general observations may be made before we come to examples. The term "non-Christian" must cover the aggressive atheist (to use an old-fashioned word), the passive agnostic, and what one takes to be the pretty large body of people who, in Charles Williams's phrase, without being themselves Christians are opposed to those who oppose Christianity. They are people who have profound reverence for the character and teaching of Christ, and profound sympathy with the Christian scale of values and the best Christian tradition, but are unable to accept the supernaturalism of the orthodox creed, however liberally that creed be reinterpreted. It may be guessed that such people form a high proportion of those engaged in the teaching and criticism of literature, and it is chiefly they—we are not concerned with imaginative writers—who may be supposed to feel the pressure of the problem of belief. It appears therefore to be in the literal sense a mainly academic problem. But I must say that I think it is also in the abstract sense a mainly academic problem, that it is not nearly so heavy a burden as a multitude of more tangible ills that afflict mankind. If it far outweighed all others, as theoretically it should, most of us would be in a bad way. No doubt those who wander between two worlds would, as persons, be happier and richer if they held a firm dogmatic faith, but, if they cannot achieve that, they must rub along as best they can. And if one must live, so to speak, on the income from unearned capital, one may prefer the capital of the Christian—and classical—inheritance to the more fluid assets of psychology. As readers and critics of Christian literature, such people may be under a partial handicap; yet the amount of great and positively Christian literature is, relatively, not large, and, moreover, a strongly sympathetic knowledge of the Christian tradition is a potent quickener of attachment and insight. To mention a less individual matter, for literature of the sixteenth and the earlier seventeenth century, including Shakespeare, modern students of all kinds have had an invaluable key, or foundation, in the Christian and classical doctrine of order and degree, which was metaphysical, religious, ethical, social, and political. Finally, these indeterminate Laodiceans may possibly be better qualified than some Christians for the understanding of non-Christian writing.

We are thinking of the literature, mainly the poetry, of the Christian era, from Dante onward. It is plain that some technical and aesthetic elements lie outside the question; we cannot distinguish between a Christian and a non-Christian prosody—it might not be irrelevant here to recall George Brandes's remark about Voltaire's verse, that the man who had little respect for anything in heaven or earth respected the uniform caesura of the Alexandrine. But some central elements of technique do lie within the problematic area; structure and language and image may depend upon Christian beliefs and ideas. For a random and simple and tremendous example, George Herbert's *Virtue* moves from everyday natural phenomena to the final conflagration of the world, the judgment day, and immortality; but the most stubbornly secular reader can hardly fail there in understanding or even in imaginative and emotional response (though a student did once raise a query about the geological formation of coal). Nor, to take a less simple case, can one imagine a reader of *Lycidas* so invincibly skeptical that he is not carried away by the beatific vision that resolves all Milton's questioning of divine providence and justice. The complexities of *Paradise Lost,* and of Dante, may be postponed.

In this connection, readers of the most diverse belief or unbelief may unite in deploring the increasing ignorance of the Bible. Last May, in my examination in Milton, I asked for a short note on the first and third temptations in *Paradise Regained,* and two students, displaying a knowledge of the Bible on a par with their knowledge of Milton, spoke of Christ's being challenged to jump off a cliff. But, lest I give an unjust impression of Harvard and Radcliffe, I hasten to add that many students are conversant with the Bible and that many respond warmly to Milton. The necessity of knowing the Bible—not to mention Christian iconography and related things—needs no proof, though it will have some illustration as we go along. I do not of course mean to suggest that for students of literature the Bible is only a primitive *Golden Bough.*

On the positive side, one general phenomenon that has a large bearing on our problem is too familiar to need description, that is, the revival of religion, or at least of interest in religion, among intellectuals. In recent decades there has been much more respectful recognition of the Christian view of life and man than conventional liberalism used to permit; and indeed one main cause of the change has been a conviction of the inadequacy or bankruptcy of that liberalism. The numerical strength of writers actually committed to the Christian faith may not be great, but among them are poets and critics and religious thinkers who cannot be brushed off as unintelligent. This movement has distinctly altered the literary climate and made sophisticated readers in general much more receptive to religious writings and ideas. Even the secular critic has added to his vocabulary—partly for the discussion of modern literature—such unwonted words as sin, guilt, redemption, nature, grace. And even if we grant the currency of more religiosity than religion, this is still significant evidence of disquietude, of dissatisfaction with liberal nostrums.

Assuming that many or most students of literature are of the non-Christian but sympathetic group already described, and that the core of the material is poetry in the Christian tradition, I should like to glance briefly at two sets of examples, first at short religious poems and later at some works of the largest scope. My remarks must be summary, and some personal reactions or guesses may be mistaken—in which case I shall no doubt be promptly informed. We might ask first how we react to the great stream of Christian lyrics that flows from the Middle Ages to the middle of the seventeenth century. Few readers, one imagines, are untouched—if they read them—by the purity and power of medieval poems, from *The Dream of the Rood* to *Quia Amore Langueo;* but what we would call their devotional naïveté may keep them outside our world of experience. To leap up to George Herbert, probably every reader divides his poems into a minor and a major category. Most of those that celebrate things ecclesiastical appeal only or mainly, in Coleridge's phrase, to "an affectionate and dutiful child of the Church," whereas Herbert's usually

greater poems are greater because they deal with worldly allure-
ments, rebellious self-will, the desire for discipline and humility
and for the renewal of spiritual energy, with conflicts and aspira-
tions and defeats and victories that belong to all human life. In
an examination in a course of mine I once asked if barriers of
belief stood between the religious metaphysicals and the modern
reader, and one particularly memorable answer came from a
Jewish student who, remarking on the very different tradition
in which he had grown up, argued that no one who wished to
live above the natural level could fail to be moved by Herbert.

I do not want to overwork Herbert, but his purely religious
poetry has a special value for this discussion; and, to report another item from the same course, it seems to me a fact of interest
that last year nearly as many undergraduates chose to write pa-
pers on Herbert as on Donne, though all Donne's secular poetry
was open to them. (Perhaps I should have some qualms about
referring to my course on the metaphysical poets because, after
this paper was written, a story in *The New Yorker* made use of
the course as a kind of nursery or backdrop for adolescent passions.) As for Donne's religious poems, they have their technical
and aesthetic interest, which is considerable but not inexhaust-
ible; yet, with a few exceptions, I do not think that, after the
first impact, they wear very well. We—I should no doubt say I
—read them less as religious poems than as further revelations of
Donne's sensibility and technique. And I would say much the
same thing of the *Anniversaries,* which Professor Martz has so
admirably analyzed; these poems seem to me for the most part
personal and historical documents rather than religious poems
that actually speak to us—as, for example, the conclusion of

Spenser's *Mutability* speaks to us. Whereas Herbert can enter into and act upon our own being, most of Donne's religious poetry remains an external object of intellectual study. I may be inviting still more violent protest if I venture to link with Donne's *Holy Sonnets* the "terrible sonnets" of Hopkins; here again we feel a powerful and painful shock, but can many of us really get inside them, or can they get inside us? And I will add that *The Windhover,* however exciting as a poem, I can feel only dimly as a religious poem; to me the central image seems not to express but to swallow up the religious theme.

Though I may have completely disqualified myself as a witness, I will proceed. If Donne is in the main too special to speak to our condition, so, in another way, is Crashaw. I cannot recall having been aware of any student of any belief or of none who did not respond to Herbert's "Love bade me welcome." I cannot recall anyone who did respond to *The Weeper* or the more flamboyant odes—a fact that may only reflect upon the expositor. On the other hand, every reader not only possesses Marvell's *Bermudas* with spontaneous ease but understands the subtle delineation of irreligious pride in *The Coronet*. It might be supposed that Vaughan's flashes of vision—quite apart from his poetic lapses—would place him in the category of poets not generally accessible to the modern reader, but I have not found it so, although he does stand somewhat farther from the center than Herbert. If the inference from all these notes and queries is not too obvious to be stated, it is that—various kinds of artistic power being taken for granted—the great poetry of religious meditation, the poetry that really comes home to modern readers who do not share the beliefs it embodies, is that which extends beyond the particular creed and personality of its author, which grows out of and embraces general human experience. And to these seventeenth-century examples might be added, for the same reason, such a rare modern work as *Four Quartets*. Even if a reader views the Christian story and Christian symbols as no more than archetypal myths, his doing so is a recognition of their experiential validity, their truth to life.

To take a wider sweep, we might now look briefly at four or five authors of major works, of whom some wrote about life in general, some almost wholly on religious themes.

One cannot imagine any creed, unless perhaps hard-boiled Marxism, that could interfere with a modern reader's wholehearted delight in Chaucer. And though Chaucer, with all his satire of ecclesiastics, was a good Catholic, there are few parts of his work where a Catholic reader has an advantage over a non-Catholic. The reasons do not need to be spelled out; it is clear that Chaucer's rich and substantial humanity transcends time and creeds. We might say that, possessing an assured faith which settled all final issues, he was free to focus his genial, unblinking gaze on men and women as they are. Yet that view would hardly explain Dante or the English Dante, Langland, and we must make large allowance for Chaucer's individual temper. And Chaucer was not always content with contemplation of the human comedy. We remember the tragic as well as the comic ironies of *Troilus,* and the moving epilogue in which the poet exhorts young fresh folks to turn from the passions of earth to the security of heavenly love.

For our problem, Dante is of course a supreme test case. Mr. Eliot recommended knowledge and understanding and the sus-

pension of both belief and disbelief—although he brought a
great deal more than that to his own reading, as indeed he acknowledged. Mr. Eliot has probably been a principal agent in
what may be called a revival of Dante, which seems to have gone
on mainly though not wholly among actual or vestigial Christians. It may at any rate be presumed that the secular reader's enjoyment progressively lessens after he leaves the *Inferno,* and
that full response to the *Paradiso* is available chiefly to the Christian. I cannot help recalling here the remark of an eminent
Christian-Platonist philosopher and sympathetic reader, A. E.
Taylor, that for most of us Dante's paradise has, at moments, an
unfortunate resemblance to a glorified firework night at the Crystal Palace. If I may, with even more candor, use myself as an ill-
starred guinea pig, I must report that, after numerous readings
over many years, I still find much of the *Divine Comedy* more
alien than Homer and Virgil and Aeschylus and Sophocles; and
I should like to think that my failure is not due entirely to inadequate command of Italian or theology or philosophy or inadequacy of belief. Doctrine that becomes bare and obtrusive may,
no doubt, awaken problems of belief that imagination had kept
quiescent, yet the exposition of doctrine is not necessarily fatal;
beliefs and ideas, passionately felt, can make superb poetry, as
in Lucretius or in Milton's passage on the old law and the gospel,
which rightly evokes in Mr. Rajan an ecstasy of admiration. Nor,
in this as in other cases, is the mere reconstruction of beliefs and
ideas an obstacle; all literature of the past necessitates the reconstruction of a multitude of secular data. The question is how far
the reasonably informed and well-disposed reader is able to enter
into a given work, and no general formula will cover individual

instincts and limitations. Since, for an infinity of readers much better equipped than I, Dante is one of the world's greatest poets, a Lilliputian arrow will not damage him, so I will go on to say that I feel a great gap between his miserable and often dehumanized sinners and his vision of divine love and order, and that what is lacking is the ethical humanity that is so central in the classical poets. Those who wish to consign me to the lowest circle of hell are anticipated by my own sentence.

That ethical humanity is central, along with religion, in Spenser, a poet whose fate it has been to be widely misread in the past as a romantic dreamer and picture-maker and in modern times to be read and understood only by scholars. Some readers avoid *The Faerie Queene* altogether because of the allegory, and some follow the romantic prescription of ignoring it, which is equally fatal. Northrop Frye remarks in his *Anatomy of Criticism* (p. 90) that the critic "often urges us to read Spenser and Bunyan . . . for the story alone and let the allegory go, meaning by that that he regards his own type of commentary as more interesting." As for storytelling, Josephine Bennett has justly observed that Spenser should be linked with Dante rather than with the romancers he sometimes imitated, Ariosto and Tasso (though of course his loose texture is closer to them than to Dante's density). It is a commonplace of literary history that all rivers of thought and poetic art flow through Spenser, and, with him as with other great poets, the more one knows the better. Yet most of *The Faerie Queene* is richly intelligible to the attentive reader who has a minimal knowledge of the beliefs, ideas, and attitudes of the Renaissance and the Reformation. The first book, of Holiness, has an archetypal structure and theme; it is linked with the

motifs of the quest and the unpromising hero, with the romance
and the morality play. As a good Anglican, Spenser was a good
Calvinist, but he was first of all a devout and compassionate
Christian, and his anti-Catholic Protestantism did not prevent
his using Catholic symbols. And while in the second book, of
Temperance, Guyon is equipped with Platonic and Aristotelian
reason, with the power of moral choice, it is in this classical book
only that an angel appears, to protect the exhausted hero. Whatever refinements of insight are provided by the reader's learning,
no problem of knowledge or belief comes between him and such
lines as

> And is there care in heaven? And is there love
> In heavenly spirits to these creatures bace,
> That may compassion of their evils move?
> There is: else much more wretched were the cace
> Of men, then beasts. . . .   (ii.viii.i)

It is in this book also that, to follow Professor Woodhouse, the
conquest of original sin is achieved, not through the power of
natural reason, but through Providence and grace.

Spenser can create a myth with the simplicity of an old wives'
tale, or with the allusive obliqueness of *The Waste Land*. Thus
at the end of Book i, when St. George, the Knight of Holiness,
has slain the dragon of evil, his merging with the figure of
Christ is indicated in unmistakable terms:

> And after to his Pallace he them brings,
> With shaumes, and trompets, and with Clarions sweet;
> And all the way the joyous people sings,
> And with their garments strowes the paved street.   (i.xii.13)

A more familiar example of the same kind is the beginning of the climactic stanza of the *Epithalamion:*

> Open the temple gates unto my love,
> Open them wide that she may enter in. . . .

Here Spenser suggests both the religious order of marriage and his reverence for his bride through a daring echo of the Twenty-fourth Psalm: "Lift up your heads, O ye gates. And be ye lift up, ye everlasting doors, and the king of glory shall come in." Spenser, by the way, and Milton likewise, differ from the early Eliot and some other modern poets both in not using private allusions and in not putting the whole weight of meaning on an allusion; the allusion is a great enrichment of meaning, but is not the sole clue. For a Miltonic example, when, after Adam has allied himself with Eve in her sin, and she exclaims "O glorious trial of exceeding love," the general irony is clear; but the phrase suggests further the contrast between her selfishness and Adam's weakness and the selfless love of Christ for man.

The case of Milton is partly parallel to Spenser's. Nineteenth-century criticism, in the romantic and liberal tradition, did not understand *Paradise Lost,* and either exalted its author as an unwitting member of the devil's party or ignored his fable and ideas altogether and listened only to the organ voice. In spite of the illuminating activities of modern scholarship and criticism, Miltonic truth is still bestuck with slanderous darts, and *Paradise Lost* has rested under a much heavier handicap than the *Divine Comedy,* though it might seem to possess some advantages. It is a great fable of the never-ending war between good and evil, humility and pride, in the world and in the heart of man; its design is simple and clear as well as vast; the poem moves with energy and speed; it has much less theology and philosophy than the *Divine Comedy;* and if it lacks ordinary human characters (and Adam and Eve become a very human Everyman and Everywoman), it does not require in running footnotes a Who's Who of medieval Europe. If it is said that Dante's style commends itself to modern poets as a model, while Milton's does not, most readers are not poets, and the colloquial is not the only good kind of style; moreover, while old-fashioned critics like Dr. Leavis see Milton as a simple-minded rhetorician splashing at a ten-league canvas with brushes of comets' hair, more discerning students have begun to recognize and analyze the subtleties of Milton's language, syntax, and rhythm—subtleties that are below the surface and were not supposed to exist in "classical" art. Since Dante's beliefs can hardly be more palatable to the modern intellectual than Milton's, and might well be less so, one suspects that some readers simply dislike Milton's personality, or alleged personality (as Mr. Eliot avowedly does), though it is doubtful if Dante's was a very sweet and pliable nature. The same charge attaches to Milton's God, who, though he can speak like a divine being, may be said to reveal a partial failure in poetic tact. Yet it seems a bit strange that a few lines from God, which, though harsh in tone, are a repudiation of Calvinism and an assertion of man's individual responsibility, should antagonize readers who are quite undisturbed by the multitudinous victims and tortures of Dante's hell.

The conventional misinterpretation of *Paradise Lost* has been kept alive partly through the inertia of unenlightened prejudice, partly through the failure to see that Milton's technique is not merely epic but dramatic. He presents characters in the way Shakespeare does, relying, as Shakespeare could rely, on the religious and ethical reactions of his audience, on the religious and ethical absolutes of general acceptance. Shakespeare, to be sure, may leave good at least outwardly defeated by evil, though his audience is left in no doubt as to which is which, and in no real doubt as to the nature of the defeat and the victory. Milton, both because he is Milton and because the epic allows direct comment, is much more positive and explicit. Thus, since evil, whatever its success, cannot ultimately overcome good, Satan and his fellows are enveloped from first to last in irony. A sufficient example is Satan's first speech of defiance, uttered when he finds Beëlzebub beside him in the lake of fire: "If thou beest he—but O how fallen. . . ." It is from this speech, and the shorter ones that follow, that romantic misinterpretation starts. Readers who automatically applaud a rebel, no matter what he is, what his motives are, or what he rebels against, see nothing but heroic grandeur in this speech, though every line of it reveals Satan's corruption as plainly as Iago's speeches reveal his; but no one has ever been naïve enough to take Iago as Shakespeare's interpreter.

If, in the present age of enlightenment, the Satanist fallacy no longer needs demonstration, Milton can supply a harder test for the non-Christian or even the Christian reader, both of whom may assume that this poet sees everything in crude black and white. After Adam's first chill of horror that follows Eve's blithe account of her sin, he speaks thus:

> O fairest of creation, last and best
> Of all God's works, creature in whom excelled
> Whatever can to sight or thought be formed,

Holy, divine, good, amiable, or sweet!
How art thou lost, how on a sudden lost,
Defaced, deflowered, and now to death devote!
Rather how hast thou yielded to transgress
The strict forbiddance, how to violate
The sacred fruit forbidden! Some cursed fraud
Of enemy hath beguiled thee, yet unknown,
And me with thee hath ruined, for with thee
Certain my resolution is to die;
How can I live without thee, how forgo
Thy sweet converse and love so dearly joined,
To live again in these wild woods forlorn? . . . .

We can notice only a couple of things here. The first four lines
are an unwitting revelation of the idolatry that will soon lead
Adam to share Eve's sin; she is not the "fairest of creation, . . .
best / Of all God's works. . . ." Eve herself has fallen through
seeking to become a goddess, but Adam had already made her
one, raising her above himself and hence above his relation to
God. In now clinging to Eve in her sin Adam is, as Gerard Man-
ley Hopkins said, falsely chivalrous, though not every reader can
whole-heartedly apply Hopkins's Christian scale of values. And
Milton himself, in implicitly condemning Adam, makes us at the
same time feel and sympathize with his human loyalty. More
than one critic has remarked on the poignant power of the lines
in which Adam's anguished imagination anticipates Eden, hitherto the perfect paradise, as, without Eve, "these wild woods
forlorn."

This rapid survey of some large works seems to lead to the
same conclusion as our glance over short religious poems:

namely, that, while we may not share the religious creeds of these poets, and while they would not be what they are if they had not held those creeds, their full and enduring appeal to us—artistic power being again taken for granted—depends upon the degree to which their vision of the world and human experience transcends particular articles of belief (and a still more cogent example might have been *Samson Agonistes*). This is, to be sure, only another truism, and one that operates no less in the purely secular sphere; those works that are tied to ephemeral themes, like some plays of Ibsen and Shaw, may fade with the fading of the causes they espoused (unless saved by other elements). But I do not mean that a poet's religious view of the world and human destiny must be reduced by criticism to nonreligious terms, must be purged of its essence, in order that the nonreligious reader may receive only the kind of ideas he prefers or is used to. I mean rather that the religious poet must himself establish enough common ground for them both to stand on. If the secular reader is to gain what may be thought a higher vision than his own, it must come—if we are sticking to literature—through a poet whose vision of perfection embraces also a vision of earth and the natural man, or, to turn things around, through a poet whose vision of earth and the natural man embraces also a vision of perfection. The proportions may of course vary widely— Chaucer and Shakespeare on the one hand, Dante and Milton on the other, and Spenser in the middle—but it is the very definition of the greatest poets, including the ancients, that they have such a simultaneous double vision. To some, Shakespeare may seem a dubious figure here, even on the less overtly religious side; yet, though we may stop well short of recent pictures of him as a dramatist of positive Christian symbolism, we cannot dispute his continual and significant Christian allusions and overtones. And though it has been said that the least touch of any theology which has a compensating heaven to offer the tragic hero is fatal, it is perhaps legitimate to think, for example, of "And flights of angels sing thee to thy rest."

I linked the ancients with the Christian poets, and they provide impressive confirmation of the argument, if any be needed. In our reading of the Greek and Latin poets, to repeat the obvious, the question of belief does not arise. Yet this body of poetry and drama remains the fountainhead of Western literature and a living possession for us not merely because of artistic greatness but mainly because its ethical values are so largely our values; we apprehend them with a directness that elements of difference cannot obscure. Moreover, while pagan religion and ethics through the centuries underwent a process of refinement not unlike that of Christianity, those ethical standards carried religious as well as human and rational sanctions. Homer's gods may at times be morally irresponsible, or even comic, but they can also guide and protect human virtue. "The blessed gods," says Eumaeus to Odysseus, "do not love wicked deeds but honor justice and the righteous acts of men." Anyhow, whatever the vagaries of the gods, Homer's ethics have an unfailing soundness and rightness. What was instinctive and practical in Homer was, much later, philosophized in the ethical psychology of Plato and, later still, in the Stoic doctrine of right reason. Both that psychology and that doctrine of right reason, which rest on accepted absolutes, were absorbed by Christianity; we may recall that famous utterance of Hooker's which begins with an assertion that may seem, from a devout Christian, rather startling: "The general and perpetual voice of men is as the sentence of God himself. . . ." Thus Christian ethics could operate in one or more of several interrelated ways, in terms of obedience to divine commands, to the conscious ethical reason, or to the instincts of common decency. All three ways are manifest in Shakespeare. If Shakespeare's religious creed is very different from Homer's, and no less his questioning of the human situation, his ethics have the same soundness and rightness. His highroad leading nowhere, as Alfred Harbage has said, is the road home; what he tells us is what we have always known—though he tells us much more too. If his tragedies lacked all Christian motives and coloring, there would be a great loss, yet their center of gravity would not be displaced; they would be inconceivably different, or rather, they would not be conceivable at all, if he were morally neutral or naturalistic.

When the slayer of Hector and the father of Hector meet, brought together by the command of Zeus, they both learn the meaning of compassion. The same lesson is learned, through suffering, by King Lear, and he dies, like the aged Oedipus, in the knowledge of love given and received. The mind of Hamlet swarms with ideas and feelings unknown to Orestes, but there are affinities between them; and if the individual revenger, heaven's scourge and minister, in some sense fails, the health of Denmark is to be restored by Fortinbras as a new kind of justice is established with the Areopagus. In both Aeschylus and Shakespeare, whatever the success of evil in the world, there is a righteous power that catches up with the wicked. And the religious integrity that unites Antigone with Jeanie Deans bridges the gulf between the laws that grow not old and the God of Scottish Calvinism. To go outside religious ethics, a young man's initiation into the adult world of evil links Sophocles's Neoptolemus with the central figure in Hemingway's *The Killers*. I do not forget the far greater heights and depths of vision and experience that Christianity brought with it, yet, in the spirit of Erasmus's "Sancte Socrates, ora pro nobis," we may say of the greatest pagan and Christian poets that they "are folded in a single party."

Implications of an Organic Theory of Poetry

It was I. A. Richards who gave us the exact phrasing of our topic, "the problem of belief." But of course he did not invent the problem. The problem dates from the beginnings of literature, and from time to time in the past literary men have been conscious of it as a problem. But our own half-century is surely the period in which theorists have bestowed most attention on it. I do not mean this observation to be necessarily a compliment to our age. Nor, on the other hand, do I regard it as one more fault of an Age of Criticism, though I am quite aware that many literary people are impatient with theorizing, defeatist about achieving solutions, and hanker after the old fleshpots of biography, personality, and literary gossip—not to mention the savory tidbits of bibliography. Theorizing has never been very popular, and in an Anglo-American civilization the temptation to muddle through and to be content with pragmatic sanctions is always strong. Be that as it may, the problem of belief is a genuine problem and it challenges our attention. Even if it should prove insoluble, we may learn something by honestly confronting it.

Let us begin with the simplest case, with the traditional theory upon which most of us were brought up, and to which many of our younger critics have returned (and from which many of our older critics have never departed). I refer to the dualism of form and content, which sees the poet as communicating certain truths through a certain form. The poet presents certain truths eloquently and persuasively, in terms of rich images and resonant harmonies.

A dualistic concept of poetic structure would seem bound to fall afoul of the problem of belief. For if the beliefs inculcated —however plausible the formal presentation—are false, or must seem false to the reader, how can he enjoy the poetry? T. S. Eliot, in a well-known passage, has put the difficulty very clearly: If "literature" exists, he argues, then "we must assume that the reader can obtain the full 'literary' or (if you will) 'aesthetic' enjoyment without sharing the beliefs of the author." For if we can only enjoy as poetry that which is in accord with our own beliefs, then literature ceases to exist except in the very limited senses in which clear and well-formed statements of our philosophy may be called poetry. But in that case, poetics has been collapsed into rhetoric, and the task of the poet is simply that of providing a rhetorical dress for our beliefs.

I labor this matter of the difficulty of the old form-content dualism for a reason. Only by understanding clearly the limitations it enforces in the matter of accordant belief can we properly sympathize with the desire of critics of our own age to seek to avoid this dualism. Whether those attempts have actually proved feasible or even promising is another matter. It is also significant that those critics who do not attempt to avoid the old bifurcation of form and content are concerned to mitigate its embarrassments with various qualifications and refinements. If poetry is no more than the eloquent presentation of the truths and values which seem proper to us, then indeed it does disappear in all the honorific senses it has worn in the past.

The obvious way in which to take poetry out of ruinous competition with science and philosophy is, of course, to deny that it has anything at all to do with truth. This is the celebrated solution undertaken by I. A. Richards. (I am thinking of his earlier works, for in the later Richards there are reservations and refinements that complicate the debonair ruthlessness of his original treatment of the problem.) Richards's way of denying the poet's commerce with truth was to insist that poetry does not make statements but only pseudo statements. Sir Philip Sidney may appear to us to have said something of the same kind: "The poet . . . nothing affirmeth, and therefore never lieth." But Sidney was actually engaged in freeing the poet from literalism in order to allow him to give us more general and philosophical truth, whereas Richards's poet was not concerned with truth at all. His task was rather to furnish therapeutic exercise for the reader's neural system and thus promote his mental health.

Let me try to indicate the precise function of poetry by means of an analogy. It is my own, but I think it not unfair. Poetry, I take the earlier Richards to be saying, does not give its reader a chart by which to negotiate the choppy and reef-beset waters of experience. Poetry, that is, does not give us the truth about reality. It reveals nothing. Rather, poetry is like a gyroscope—one of those great rotating devices used to keep the ship on an even keel and therefore handle the better as it makes its difficult voyage. To pursue the analogy: Richards's further point was that what we needed were stabilizing gyroscopes rather than additional charts; besides, charts could be supplied only by science.

The difficulties with Richards's position were obvious, and various critics were prompt to point them out. I shall comment upon only one of them. By locating the values of poetry in certain alleged psychological effects in the reader, Richards severed the connection between the text of the poem and any critical account of it. As John Crowe Ransom put the difficulty: what was the use of the critic's concerning himself with the form of the poem if there was no *necessary* connection between that form and its psychological effects upon the reader? The text of a poem could be inspected, but the alleged goings-on in the reader's neural system could not be. Fortunately of course, Richards had in fact a great deal to say about the form and shape of the poem—even in his earliest period—and his concern for the way in which actual readers read and misread particular poems has proved one of the fruitful influences on modern criticism. Indeed it has been remarked again and again that the influence of Richards has exerted itself not to develop an affective criticism but on the contrary has stimulated a cognitive criticism. Richards's most brilliant pupil, William Empson, made the point emphatically in his last book, *Complex Words*. So also did Murray Krieger more recently in his *New Apologists for Poetry*. But in this most fruitful and interesting aspect of his work, Richards can hardly avail himself of the easy solution of the problem of belief promised in his initial works.

Max Eastman is another writer who takes poetry out of competition with science and philosophy by denying that poetry has to do with truth. Poetry is simply "the pure attempt to heighten

cf. Poe

consciousness. Its function is to give us an awareness of the concrete world known to the senses, to make us fully conscious of
the qualities of experience. Eastman's is a primitive theory of
poetry, and it was invoked to justify a simple lyrical poetry. (Most
of the prominent names in twentieth-century poetry have been
roundly damned by Eastman for membership in what he has
called the "cult of unintelligibility.) Eastman never really succeeds in showing why there is not a greater heightened consciousness in actually eating an apple rather than in reading a poem
about eating an apple, or in sporting with a real Amaryllis in the
shade rather than in reading Milton's poem about it. Because
of his *simpliste* notions, the idealizing and reshaping which always occurs in the poem is neglected in favor of its pure sensual
intensity. Moreover, Eastman's way of dealing with the poetry of
ideas—for he does concede that there can be such a poetry—is
simple to the point of crudity. If the poet must write about ideas,
Eastman counsels him to go to an accredited scientist and get
some verified ideas to write about. The "poetry" in this case
will presumably consist of simply fleshing out the ideas with
sensuous and concrete details. We are back then to the old dualism in which science and philosophy supply the content and poetry
the decorative form.

A much more sophisticated treatment of poetry's heightening of
consciousness is to be found in Ransom's theories. But with Ransom the claim for poetry is not a denial that poetry gives us truth
but rather a proud claim that poetry *does* give truth—that it is
a special form of cognitive discourse which complements that of
science.

In a now famous essay, Ransom distinguishes three kinds of

poetry: physical poetry, which attempts to give us the thinginess of things, the concrete world of the senses; second, Platonic poetry, a poetry of ideas in which images have been reduced to the status of illustrations for the idea; and third, metaphysical poetry, in which idea and image assume a special and unique relationship. What is that relationship? It is not easy to say. Ransom's own metaphors are suggestive, rather than definitive. Later, in his volume *The New Criticism,* Ransom did attempt a definition. The ideas gave knowledge of relationships, the kind of knowledge which we find, for example, in science. These ideas determine the *structure* of a poem. But the world that we experience is a world of rich and manifold contingency, never adequately expressed in our schematizations, but only through images. This is the world that poetry is able to render more justly by its fidelity to *local texture.* Poetry then gives us a kind of double knowledge: not merely the knowledge of relationships such as that provided by science and philosophy, but in addition a knowledge of the world of experience as we experience it.

This scheme seems attractive, but I confess that I do not clearly understand it—specifically, the relation of structure to texture. In Ransom's account of the way in which structure and texture pull against each other, perhaps to yield a special perspective of vision, there are hints of a kind of tensional aesthetics; yet in some of his other statements, the structure-texture distinction looks ominously like the old content-form dualism. Moreover, Ransom's failure to reissue the book, now published some fourteen years ago, makes one hesitate to assume that the view of poetry stated in *The New Criticism* is actually one which he now holds. But going on the evidence that we have, Ransom does not seem to have advanced beyond the claim made by the old dualism that there must be a certain measure of accordant belief on the part of the reader. True, his physical poetry is dedicated to giving us the world of experience, and physical poetry raises no serious problem of belief. But the more important poems do involve ideas and it seems plain that they make use at their peril of ideas which Ransom regards as false or inadequate. Whatever the relationship of ideational structure to sensuous texture, those ideas had better be sound. In *The New Criticism,* Ransom was very clear on this point:

> I can see no necessity for waiving the intellectual standards on behalf of poets. If Dante's beliefs cannot be accepted by his reader, it is the worse for Dante with that reader, not a matter of indifference as Eliot has argued. If Shelley's argument is foolish, it makes his poetry foolish. In my mind Dante's beliefs are very bold speculations at which the accusing finger has pointed steadily for a long time now, but substantively are better grounded, and methodologically far more consistent, than Shelley's beliefs. That consideration would enter into my preference of Dante over Shelley.[1]

One could cite other passages in Ransom which would qualify and even partially contradict this swinging assertion of the importance of accordant belief. Even so, Ransom's developed position seems clearly to demand that the reader be in substantial agreement with his author. The poet as truth-teller certainly assumes a more dignified posture than the poet as purveyor of pleasing lies or pleasing nonsense. But if Dante's poetry suffers from

---

[1] *The New Criticism* (Norfolk, Conn., 1941), p. 208.

Dante's inadequate knowledge, then I suspect that the poetry of
the past will have to be constantly downgraded as more light
breaks upon us.

As another theorist who holds that poetry is cognitive, Yvor
Winters invites consideration at this point. If Ransom's position
resembles at certain points that of Max Eastman, it has at other
points affiliations with that of Winters, to whose work Ransom
has paid the compliment of serious and careful analysis. But
whereas in Ransom the old dualism between form and content
tends to be hidden, with Yvor Winters it is quite overt. Indeed
the dualism is so clearly assumed that the question will be
whether Winters is really able to avail himself of any of the ad
vantages of a theory of organic form. Winters, to be sure, is
careful to argue that poetry does more than give propositional
truth. Though it makes a "statement," the poet's statement differs
from "statements of a purely philosophical or theoretical nature, in that it has by intention a controlled content of feeling."
The element of feeling in poetry thus is important and provides the differentia that separate poetry from prose, but the
content of feeling is to be rigorously controlled and supervised by
the "rational content." Indeed, as Winters puts it, "the relationship between rational statement and feeling" is that of the "motive
to emotion." Winters's principal attack upon romantic poetry is
that the feeling in such poetry is vague and uncontrolled, and
that the modern poets, including Eliot, Pound, and Hart Crane
—incurable Romantics that they are, whatever their modern or
classical pretensions—are guilty of chaotic and unmotivated emotions. Such poets have tried to do without rational structure, and

their poetry suffers from incoherence. It lacks rational coherence and it lacks coherence of feeling too.

With Winters the problem of belief becomes acute, even though he attempts to mitigate the severity of his moralism by arguing that after all most men do have the same *basic* notions about conduct. As he observes in his *Primitivism and Decadence,*

> the fundamental concepts of morality are common to intelligent men regardless of theological orientation, except in so far as morality may be simply denied or ignored. . . . It would be difficult, I think, to find a devotional poem of which most of the implications were not moral and universal.[2]

There is certainly a measure of admirable common sense here, particularly if we take it as a counsel not to insist upon our theological differences when we read poetry. But in practice Winters himself makes much of philosophical and theological differences. He finds their effects on poetry to be extremely important. For example, to most of us, T. S. Eliot will seem a sturdy—to some of us, even a forbidding—moralist. Yet Winters indicts Eliot's poetry for its "limp" rhythms which reflect, he says, Mr. Eliot's own limp spirituality. As this last comment suggests, Winters believes in an organic theory of literature, an organic theory of sorts; but the soul of the work—to use Aristotle's phrase—is the moral judgment.

Intellect versus emotion, content versus form, the abstract principle versus its concrete vesture—these oppositions are hard to avoid. They are dualisms that seem natural to us: they accord

---

[2] *Primitivism and Decadence* (New York, 1937), p. 11.

with our ingrained habits of thinking about discourse. But unless we can avoid such a dualism in our account of poetry, we shall have difficulty in claiming for the poet any role higher than that of the mere rhetorician. We shall find it hard to counter the charge that poetry is merely an inferior kind of philosophy—unless indeed we are willing to concede that it has nothing to do, and need have nothing to do, with truth. I put the matter in this fashion in the hope that we may better understand the impulse that has made so many in our time attempt to describe the structure of poetry in other terms.

The primary motive for avoiding the form-content dualism, however, was not a desire to solve the problem of belief; theorists primarily wanted to devise a description of poetry that would fit the facts. A good poem seemed more than a skillful rhetorical packaging of some propositional truth. Form and content were indeed inseparable. The truth which the poem enunciated could with great difficulty be disentangled from the total experience that was the poem. The well-advertised "messages" or "statements" that purported to represent the core of the poem looked suspiciously like propositions abstracted from the poem, and, in the light of the rich substantiality of the poem, appeared to be fragments and even distortions of its full meaning.

On the side of form, moreover, the tropes, the decorative glozings, the various formal elements proved, in the authentic poem, to be much more than mere ornament. They had a great deal to do with what the poem "said." The interrelation of parts that one found in Marvell's *Horatian Ode* or Pope's *Rape of the Lock* or Keats's *Ode to a Nightingale* was organic—not a relation like that of brick with brick or girder with girder, but more nearly like that of cell with cell in a living organism. Such a poem seemed to deny the commonly assumed duality between form and content as these terms are commonly used and, if one wished to do justice to its special kind of unity, to demand another kind of description.

Critics of quite various persuasions have noted this kind of structure as an empirical fact. I. A. Richards, for example, even while arguing that the value of a poem was to be sought, not in its makeup, but in the psychological reaction of its reader, was actually directing our attention to the subtle interconnections of the structure of poetic meaning.

The poem seemed to be best described as a verbal context whose meaning resisted expression in any simple proposition—and indeed resisted complete expression in any abstract statement whatsoever. For the meaning was that of a total experience and included not merely intellectual elements but emotional elements as well. It was not so much a "statement" of a generalization as a "dramatization" of a particular situation. An element of tension among valuations and attitudes not easily reconciled might be an important part of the meaning. The total meaning was a complex built up out of partial meanings. Not only that: the parts of the work, including the individual words that made it up, had their individual meanings, altered by the pressure of the whole context. Whether or not one called that alteration an *ironical* qualification, or, discovering that the term *irony* was likely to mislead, used some other term, the fact of alteration was there.

This contextual conception of the poem was not, I have said, devised for the sake of dealing with the problem of belief, but rather to account for the character of poetic organization as it was empirically discovered. But the implications for the problem of belief were, and are, considerable.

If there is no "message"—no proposition—that adequately sums up what the poem is "saying," then the question as to whether one agrees with the truth of what the poem is saying becomes difficult to decide. More adequate summaries of course, may be devised. By adding reservations and making the proper qualifications, one can approximate an adequate summary of what the poem "says." But this very process of expanding the statement and providing shadings and qualifications of its meaning made some of us question whether this way of arriving at the truth of the poem was not one that violated the very nature of poetry. Perhaps propositional truth was not altogether commensurate with poetic truth.

One way in which to put the implications of a contextual theory of poetry is to say that it shifts the emphasis from truth of correspondence to truth of coherence. The critic finds himself talking less about the correspondence of the poem to reality than about the coherence among the parts of the poem. Indeed, he may find himself saying, as I have often found myself saying, that a prime way in which a poem failed was that it presented a proposition to the reader so directly that the poem became a mere preachment, sacrificing density and substantiality achieved through coherence, to mere correspondence. This error is Poe's "didactic heresy," though many other poets, including Shelley, have condemned a naked didacticism. To come down to our own times: didacticism is Ransom's "Platonic" poetry in which the images, no longer wild but ignominiously tamed, are reduced to illustrations in the service of the dominant idea.

Yet, granted the importance of truth of coherence in poetry, is such truth sufficient? Must there not also be a truth of correspondence between the views incorporated in a poem and the reality of human experience? Granted that, if the answer be "yes," we may have some difficulty in avoiding the limitation of "good" poetry to that that flatters our own views; still, if the answer be "no," has not poetry won its independence at the terrible price of having detached itself from reality?

But before we are driven to answer yes or no, we need to consider the nature of poetry once more. In the first place, a poem is something made, a construct. A renewed consciousness of a poem as an object—an artifact—and with that a renewed respect for craftsmanship, have been salient traits of twentieth-century literary theory, especially with such writers as T. E. Hulme, T. S. Eliot, and Ezra Pound. Such has also been the stress of theorists of fiction like Henry James and Ford Maddox Ford. This respect for the thing made and for the craft that goes into the making have gone hand in hand with a humility and self-effacement on the part of the maker. His art became more than an outpouring of personality—or an imposition of his own ideas upon limp and passive materials. Rather the process of composition has been conceived of as one of experimentation and exploration—a testing of insights against the funded experience of the race as contained in, and refracted through, language. Composition included an element of struggle with a resisting medium; hence the recalcitrant nature of dramatic truth. There was also an element of submission: the making involved the acceptance of something from without, and was no mere action of the conscious will. The relation resembled that once celebrated in the myth of the muse.

Modern psychology suggested another terminology, a submission of one's consciousness to the darker subliminal forces of one's own mind. But neither the classic nor the modern myth was required to account for the empirical fact.

The way in which Eliot—though no Jungian—has sometimes written about the process of composition has prompted Yvor Winters to wonder whether Eliot is not assuming what he calls "an automatic, or unconscious art, an art which is an extreme form of romantic mysticism." Indeed, Winters has sardonically summarized Eliot's doctrine of composition thus: "the artist does not really know what he is doing; a doctrine which . . . leads directly to the plainest kind of determinism." [3] But this passage represents Winters in his most vindictive mood, the moral cop on the beat, whanging the feet of the man sprawled on the bench and saying: "No slumping down here, my good man, and let's have no whining about it."

But Eliot was not arguing that a poem simply bubbles up out of the unconscious as a pure response to some accidental stimulus. What he was saying was that poems are fashioned, and that the "material" out of which they are fashioned offers a certain resistance—a resistance that may lead to discoveries. The material is language, not as the Chicago School of critics seems to consider language, a merely phonetic protoplasm without inherent character, but, as I should put it, an incarnate symbolism in which sense datum and idea, concept and valuation, are interfused and where meaning jostles meaning. If this medium promises to clothe any naked idea dipped into it, it also threatens in the process to transform the idea. The language embodies in some

[3] *The Anatomy of Nonsense* (Norfolk, Conn., 1943), p. 122.

real sense the funded experience of the race. For this reason, the recalcitrance of language may well be fruitful; for it demands that the idea be reconciled to the world of sense and contingency, which is the difficult and tangled world that we know in our mundane experience.

Here is William Butler Yeats dealing with an aspect of this notion. Yeats is writing to the playwright Sean O'Casey, cautioning him against imposing upon his plays his own opinions as a man:

> Among the things that dramatic action must burn up are the author's opinions; while he is writing he has no business to know anything that is not a portion of that action. Do you suppose for one moment that Shakespeare educated Hamlet and King Lear by telling them what he thought and believed? As I see it, Hamlet and Lear educated Shakespeare, and I have no doubt that in the process of that education he found out that he was an altogether different man to what he thought himself, and had altogether different beliefs. A dramatist can help his characters to educate him by thinking and studying everything that gives them the language they are groping for through his hands and eyes, but the control must be theirs, and that is why the ancient philosophers thought a poet or dramatist Daimon-possessed.[4]

Allen Tate makes a related point in an early essay where he distinguishes between metaphor imposed by the poet upon an experience in order to "explain" it and metaphor which seems to grow out of the experience. His illustration is the figure "Ripe-

[4] *The Letters of W. B. Yeats,* ed. by Allan Wade (New York, 1955), p. 741.

makes a moral judgment, though I believe that he is more heavy-handed than it is wise to be. I see no need of collapsing the ethical and aesthetic realms.

What the author and the various readers of a work do need to hold in common, I would suggest, is not so much the same set of beliefs about the universe as the same set of general human responses. We can participate in the same piece of literature even though we may differ considerably in our philosophical positions; but we can scarcely be said to participate in the play *Macbeth,* if we differ about, say, the credibility of Macbeth's response to a given situation or the adequacy of the motives that cause him to undertake a certain action. Readers must agree that the artist succeeds in making, or that he fails to make, his characters convincing; and beyond that, they must share a criterion to which that judgment of success or failure can be appealed—the pattern of *human* nature that exists within us, and which must surely be the most relevant part of that *nature* which was for Alexander Pope "At once the source and test and end of Art."

If this pattern of human nature is indeed within us and within all of us, it may seem gratuitous to call attention to it. Yet there is the danger that our present-day awareness of cultural diversity and the claims of cultural relativism may obscure for us the importance of the basis upon which our participation in literature rests. If man in his essential humanity does not exist, and if his unchanging fundamental oneness does not transcend the innumerable differences that set apart individual men and men of various cultures and periods of history, then I do not think that we can talk about poetry at all. Unless we can assume that Man in this sense does exist, we necessarily abandon any concept of an aesthetics of poetry in favor of a tabulation of various kinds of personal and social expression.

In short, if the primary structural relationship in poetry is coherence and not correspondence, then our criterion for judging coherence becomes of first importance, and this is, I suggest, our basic pattern of human nature, not necessarily as reshaped by Freud or Adler, or as summarized in some textbook, but a living pattern actually experienced. For the coherence of parts in a literary work depends upon our belief in the plausibility of certain human actions and reactions, responses and valuations. In these we must "believe" or the work of art is indeed incredible and monstrous. That such a picture of human nature has definite implications for nature in general—for reality itself —I should be the first to acknowledge. But the correspondence to reality that a poem achieves is mediated through its special kind of structure. And that fact has to be given due weight.

The sins committed by the artist in his specific character as artist, I am going to suggest, are best described as violations of coherence: the exploitation of the sentimental, of the merely sensational, of the monstrous, and in general all obfuscations of human perception and action. It is tempting to add to these sins the clinical and the pornographic presentations, for these too are faults that the writer falls into by failing to obey the demand for full coherence. And the reader, in his turn, mistaken about the role of literature, may be willing to accept the clinical, the mere case history, instead of the "complete" and value-suffused knowledge of a human experience; or, mistaken in another way, he may believe that the function of literature is to deal with feelings in a narrow context or indeed without reference to any fully human context at all, so that the play on the feelings becomes a direct stimulation for its own sake. The light that literature sheds is indirect lighting: it is not the hard direct light by which the surgeon plies his scalpel or that which floodlights an advertisement on night display.

The particular bearing of violations of coherence upon the matter of belief deserves a little illustration. The *Antigone* of Sophocles ought, one would think, to raise very serious problems of belief. Sophocles inherited a religious and philosophical position very different from our own. If the historian of ideas can point to certain continuities, he does in fact point to a myriad of differences. Indeed, we may be so overawed at the differences that we feel that literary values are only relative after all.

Yet it is a matter of fact that modern readers can appreciate *Antigone* as a piece of literature and can make meaningful comparisons between it as drama and the dramas of William Shakespeare or Thomas Otway or Tennessee Williams. Burial customs have changed radically since the time of the kingdom of Thebes as Sophocles imagined it. Indeed we may need a footnote from the historian of Greek culture to understand why Antigone feels it is so urgent that she sprinkle a handful of dust over her brother's corpse. But once the note has been supplied, her action becomes to us deeply and admirably human and her fate tragic. If she is an exalted being, she is nevertheless a credible human being.

The characters created by Tennessee Williams, on the other hand, I often find to be quite incredible. Ostensibly they live in our twentieth-century world and hold views of reality that

are familiar to many of us, but I have great difficulty in believing in some of their actions. For example, in *The Rose
Tattoo,* I simply find it impossible to believe that Serafina delle
Rose would say some of the things she does say or do some of
the things that she is made to do. And even when I can credit
a certain action of hers as possible, I cannot connect it with the
actions that precede and follow it. To me the play is funda-
mentally incoherent, though I can understand how audiences
that are hungry for immediate and sensational theatricality may
be quite willing to waive all considerations of dramatic proba-
bility, or how they may argue that the actions, implausible
though they may seem, are really true, since the play must be
sociologically sound. Here the argument shifts from truth of
coherence to truth of correspondence with a vengeance. The
play becomes for such auditors, and not without an encouraging
nudge from Mr. Williams, a rubberneck bus tour through the
depraved provinces. What cannot be validated artistically is to
be validated by an appeal to the psychiatrist or to the sociologist.

And now for a more positive illustration. Shakespeare's suicides
do not trouble most Christians, even Christians who make a
full commitment to their religion and regard suicide as a
mortal sin that allows no opportunity for repentance. The young
and passionate lovers, Romeo and Juliet, kill themselves, but
so do also those more mature and worldly and less impetuous
lovers, Antony and Cleopatra.

Romeo and Juliet in their actions show a blend of folly and
nobility, of rashness and of tender concern for the loved one.
But Romeo and Juliet are not doctrinaire exponents of a special
moral code, nor on the other hand candidates for some psy-

chiatrist's casebook. Their motivations are mixed and are intimately related to the mixed world of good and evil in which they have their being. In reading the play, the knowledge that we gain of the characters is intimately connected with an increased knowledge of our selves. That knowledge is not coldly clinical nor is it morbidly curious, the knowledge of something monstrous and freakish. Even fantasy and satire, I would maintain, yield a knowledge that is, in William Faulkner's phrase, "knowledge carried to the heart."

Characteristically, this knowledge of the springs of the actions of Romeo and Juliet does not necessarily carry with it our moral approval. Our pity for their blindness may be quite as strong as our admiration. So also with the suicides of Antony and Cleopatra—whose world is so different from that of Shakespeare's Verona and whose characters counterpoise the passionate youth of the younger lovers with the sophistication and even the cunning of middle age. But in poetry, to understand everything is not necessarily to forgive everything. We are beyond that facile observation, for neither condemnation nor forgiveness is in question. What Shakespeare has done in *Antony and Cleopatra* has been to dramatize the situation so accurately, so honestly, and with such fidelity to all the claims of the situation that it is no longer a question of our belief in the innocence or guilt of the two royal lovers, but of our participation in the poetic experience. The experience of the play certainly has a relation to our notions of ethics. It will test our ethical notions. It will probably deepen our sympathies and at the same time deepen our sense of man's responsibilities as a moral agent. But the play does not pretend to be an eloquent presentation of the proper ethical principle or the argument for a particular choice: rather it carries us deep into the crucial experience which conditions any choice.

The knowledge that poetry yields is given indirectly and even circuitously. But I would not have my own account of this process appear so circuitous as to seem evasive. Though the problem of definition is troublesome, I do not want to evade it. Let me tend toward a conclusion therefore with a little sheaf of scattered observations—some of them frankly metaphorical, some of them borrowed from others, and perhaps not all of them to be completely reconciled with another.

Poetry does yield knowledge of the human situation, but it tends to give diagnoses rather than remedies. It may be useful to man's moral health, for an adequate remedy will probably depend upon a sound diagnosis. But there may be more than one remedy, and in any case a remedy involves an overt action whereas a diagnosis is still close to pure contemplation, which is the proper realm of art.

A poem focuses itself on a concrete situation and does not issue in an ethical generalization. The evaluation is there, but to borrow a term from the archaeologists, it is there *in situ* and can no more easily than the quick-to-crumble artifact be removed by a process of abstraction. At least one must be gentle and cautious.

William Butler Yeats is more nearly right than Matthew Arnold in holding that poetry is a revelation of life rather than a criticism of life, though one is willing to concede that any revelation implies an evaluation and thus a potential criticism.

If poetry may be said to hold up the mirror to nature, then it is a very special kind of mirror, for there is anything but a simple and direct reflection. It is more accurately viewed as a distortion mirror, or as a lens, or perhaps better still, as my colleague W. K. Wimsatt has put it, as a crystal:

> A refraction of light through a crystal tells us something about the light, something about the crystal; the refraction itself is a kind of reality, interesting to observe. Let us say that poetry is a kind of reality refracted through subjective responses. This refraction itself is an area of reality. Does the refraction tell us something unique and profound about the reality beyond itself? We need not actually say much about this for the purposes of a workable poetics. (Much will depend on what we conceive the ultimate character of that reality to be.) [6]

Because the reality treated by poetry is a reality refracted through human responses, the revelation that poetry makes is primarily a revelation of ourselves, and the primary criterion to which it must appeal its judgments is some norm of the human psyche. Poetry is man-centered in a very special way. It transcends the limitations of the human mind at its peril— whether it be John Milton writing *Paradise Lost* or the science-fictionalist writing about Buck Rogers in the year 2200.

The kind of truth that poetry gives will rarely satisfy the propagandist, the man with a cause, the perfervid moralist, or anyone concerned with a burning issue. Poetic truth is too general, too provisional, too far removed from propositional

[6] W. K. Wimsatt, Jr., and Cleanth Brooks, *Literary Criticism: A Short History* (New York, 1957), pp. 737–78.

truth. (Eliot, one remembers, was content to ask no more than that the world view provided by the poem be coherent, mature, and founded on the facts of experience.) But these very handicaps make poetic truth available to a great many people whose professed beliefs differ widely. There may be an analogy here to a natural theology as distinguished from a theology based upon revelation. Like natural theology, poetry is more humble in its claims and proposes to found itself on the common domain of human experience. (One should, of course, add that, again like natural theology, the "truth" of poetry may be quite compatible with a truth of far more specific and more imperious claims, a truth which goes beyond it and completes poetic truth.)

The concessions that I have just made about the nature of poetic truth may well prompt someone to say, "but such truth is too vague and provisional to live by." I should agree. Though I think that poetry has a unique function and a very important function, I am not one of those people who believe that man can live by poetry alone. There is, it scarcely needs to be said, scientific truth, and there is, I should add, religious truth.

Indeed, as Mr. Abrams has reminded us in his paper, our preoccupation with the problem of belief goes back through I. A. Richards to Matthew Arnold who, confronted with a crisis in belief in his own time, tried the heroic expedient of assigning to poetry the burden that he felt religion could no longer bear. You remember the famous passage:

> Our religion has materialized itself in the fact, in the supposed fact; it has attached its emotion to the fact, and now the fact is failing it. . . . Poetry attaches its emotion to

the idea; the idea *is* the fact. . . . [More and more we will have to turn to poetry] to interpret life for us, to console us, to sustain us. Without poetry, our science will appear incomplete; and most of what now passes with us for religion and philosophy will be replaced by poetry.[7]

Small wonder that the problem of belief takes on a special urgency when we demand that poetry interpret life for us as religion in the past has done. My own feeling is that the attempt to substitute poetry for religion is bound to result in a real distortion of poetry and nothing better than an ersatz religion. Those who cannot accept a religion will, I should think, simply have to do without one. But I have no special competence to discuss the availability of religion to modern man. I refer to Arnold's prophecy only for the sake of making two points having to do with our problem of poetic belief.

The first is that the recent critics who have been most concerned to maintain the autonomy of poetry against the scientist, and sometimes against the Christian moralist—protesting against either its being depressed into mere instrumentality or its being inflated into a kind of mythic quasi-religious dynamic—are frequently, though surely not invariably, critics who have a definite religious commitment. As such, they have the less temptation to make poetry the source of, or the instrumentality for, transmitting the ultimate values. But I offer this comment not as self-congratulation but as a modest historical note which may explain what some observers have felt to be an anomaly of modern criticism: that the defenders of the autonomy of poetry

[7] "The Study of Poetry," *Essays in Criticism: Second Series* (London, 1921), pp. 1–3.

ought "logically" to be art-for-art's-sake men, and yet obviously are not—or are so only in the sense in which Mr. Abrams has admirably qualified this term in his paper.

My second point is a more general one. It is simply this: that Eliot was surely right a few years ago in observing that we are still living in the Age of Arnold. In terms of the issue of poetic belief we are indeed. Most critics today, including, for instance, our popular reviewers and the new "myth" critics, are pretty clearly Arnoldians, even if unconsciously so. Though I have been delighted by the measure of agreement that we seem to have arrived at—or do my eyes dazzle?—I do not delude myself that the problem can soon be counted as "settled." The problem of belief will continue to concern us, I predict, until many more of us have come closer to a solution of some of the basic questions relating to science and poetry and religion that troubled the great Victorian critic.

WALTER J. ONG, S.J.

Voice as Summons for Belief

Memory believes before knowing remembers. Believes
longer than recollects, longer than knowing even wonders.
—William Faulkner, *Light in August*

Everything that we believe, we believe either through sight
or through hearing. Sight is often deceived, hearing serves
as guaranty.
—St. Ambrose, *Commentary on St. Luke*

A Presence is never mute.
—Pierre Teilhard de Chardin, S.J., unpublished notes

Any discussion of literature and belief must at some
point enter into the mystery of voice and words. In a sense,
everyone of man's works is a word. For everything that man
makes manifests his thought. A dwelling or a spear tip com-
municates even when communication is not particularly intended.
A building or a tool, we say, "shows" thought. In this, it is
a kind of word, a saying of what is in one's mind.

In the fine arts, communication is even more intense, for the
raison d'être of works of the fine arts is some sort of com-

munication. As a "word," a painting may be polysemous and mysterious. Yet it remains something that some person has projected outside himself and made accessible to others. It externalizes something conceived within the artist—although not fully conceived, indeed until it was in some way externalized—in order that this something may be assimilated into another or others, or at least may be available for such assimilation.

In this a painting is both like and unlike a word. For, if a word is an externalization, it is not so external as this. A word can live only while actually issuing from the interior, physical and psychic, of the living individual. As soon as it has passed to the exterior, it perishes. Returning toward its speaker, a word is not a word, but only an echo. "Words, after speech, reach / Into the silence." No spoken word can exist in its entirety all at once, but only bit by bit.

On the other hand, in so far as words are formed within us, they are destined for externalization. One might conjecture about intelligences with ineffable private words which forever remain media of interior contemplation and cannot be projected to the exterior. But the fact is that our natural interior words or concepts are not of this sort. It we can conceive a thought within ourselves, it is the sort of thing our fellows—the more perceptive ones, anyhow—can enter into. If we can think it, others can, too. Depth analysis has made it more evident than ever that there is no private language, even of inarticulate symbols. In so far as we speak to ourselves in any way, others are capable of sharing our thoughts. To conceive something interiorly is to process it for externalization.

If a painting is in some sense a human word, an exterior saying of something conceived interiorly, much more is a work of literature a word. For it is not only, as a totality, a word, but the stuff of which it is compounded is words. The canvas and oils and ground clays and salts with which a painter works are not of themselves means of expression, although they can be made so. But the words with which a speaker or writer works are themselves means of expression, and, no matter what we do with them, this they must remain.

This fact, banal enough in itself, is occluded by our present tendency to think of literary works as objects. Under one of their aspects, they are objects, of course. As a painting or sculpture or even a dwelling, while essentially an object, is also in a more subtle sense a word, so a literary work, while consisting of words and being in its own totality a word, is also in a more subtle sense an object. But it is well to remind ourselves how subtle this sense really is. Would an illiterate society, where literary works could be given no vicarious existence in space through writing or printing, be able to think easily of literary works as objects?

In a society where the only known word is the pure, evanescent spoken word it is easier to think of objects as words than it is to think of words as objects. This is the mentality revealed in the Old Testament and even in the New. It is the mentality of the primitive peoples studied by Benjamin Lee Whorf and others. Even in John Donne's day, when typography was established but had not laid so tight a hold on society as it has in the days of Neo-Scholasticism and the New Criticism, a poem, circulated in manuscript, was associated with rhetoric rather than with an artifact. Literature was expression. "The play's the thing," says

Hamlet. But it is not a "thing" in the sense of an object. It is a "thing" to move the "conscience of the King." Moving or persuading was one of the offices of rhetoric.

I

When we say a literary work is a "word," we mean that it is something which is said or spoken. In our typographical culture, of course, this saying or speaking must be understood in a special sense. For in such a culture the greater bulk of literary production never finds its way out of the silence of the manuscript or the printed page. Probably the only persons who actually pronounce aloud the words of novels or of most poems written today are proofreaders, whose experience while reading proof, whatever else it may be, is hardly literary. And, alas, most of what is written never gets so far as the proofreading stage. Nevertheless, in an acceptable sense silent writing is a form of speaking, as silent reading is a form of hearing.

Speaking and hearing are not simple operations. Each exhibits a dialectical structure which mirrors the mysterious depths of man's psyche. As he composes his thoughts in words, a speaker or writer hears these words echoing within himself and thereby follows his own thought, as though he were another person. Conversely, a hearer or reader repeats within himself the words he hears and thereby understands them, as though he were himself two individuals. This double and interlocking dialectic, so beautifully described by Louis Lavelle in *La parole et l'écriture,* provides the matrix for human communication. The speaker listens while the hearer speaks.

The fact that the speaker listens to himself and the hearer

speaks to himself shows that communication is not effected between individuals related to one another as we might imagine a broadcasting station and a receiving set to be. In wireless transmission there is a center of emission and a center of reception, one active, the other passive, and there is movement of impulses from one to the other. Because it has this simple structure, broadcasting is not at all communication in the human sense. It is an aid, a tool of communication. In the human situation, matters are quite different. The center of emission is a kind of receiving center, too, and cannot emit its words properly unless it is at the same time receiving them. Similarly, the receiving center has to be a kind of center of emission, for it receives its words by imagining them as emitted. One consequence of this is that it is fallacious to imagine that words are capable of being reduced to impulses.

Every human word implies not only the existence—at least in the imagination—of another to whom the word is uttered, but it also implies that the speaker has a kind of otherness within himself. He participates in the other to whom he speaks, and it is this underlying participation which makes communication possible. The human speaker can speak to the other precisely because he himself is not purely self, but is somehow also other. His own "I" is haunted by the shadow of a "thou" which it itself casts and which it can never exorcize. In *The Secret Sharer*, that strangely existentialist story from a pre-existentialist age, Conrad's hero is painfully aware that the refugee from justice whom he has secreted on board his ship is his double, a symbol of his own interior division and of his alienation from himself. The stranger-double is somehow there in the captain's own cabin because the captain himself feels himself a stranger on his own ship, and this because he is a stranger to himself in his own soul. The same double is party to the captain's conversations with other men. When a visitor from another ship, come aboard to look for the refugee, speaks too low, the captain explains, *"As . . . I wanted my double* [concealed in the cabin] *to hear every word,* I hit upon the notion of informing him [the visitor] that I regretted to say that *I was hard of hearing"* (italics added). It was essential that the double participate secretly in the conversation. But to effect this participation, the captain had to attest a deficiency in his own powers of communication.

Conrad's profoundly symbolic tale is a kind of allegory of human existence. It reveals a rift, a limitation inside our own beings, but a rift which is our only hope of salvation—it is a rift which comes from our bearing vicariously within ourselves the other with whom we must commune, and who must commune with us, too, and thereby compensate for the rift, the limitation, in our persons. The other within must hear all, for he already knows all, and only if this other, this *thou,* hears will *I* become comprehensible to myself.

A literary work can never get itself entirely dissociated from this I-thou situation and the personal involvement which it implies. For a literary work to exist in the truest sense, it does not suffice that there be code marks, which we know as letters, printed on paper. A drawing can exist on paper, in space, in a way in which a literary work cannot. A drawing can be assimilated in an instant, at a glance. For a literary work to be what it really is, words must move in sequence, *one after another,* in someone's consciousness. The work must be read or heard, recreated in terms of communication touching an existent person or persons over a stretch of time.

The manner of this literary communication is, of course, complex in the extreme. As compared with real dialogue between two persons, a literary performance—a story or a poem or a play—has a special objective quality, signalized by the fact that the author himself stands outside the work, as Shakespeare's own person stands outside his plays. In this way the literary work is like a drawing. It is in a sense something that the author has extruded and thereupon left. This same impression is not given by the words spoken in a personal conversation in which persons find themselves actually involved through the process of daily living. The words in such conversation are less exteriorized.

The symbol of the exteriority of a literary creation is the mask, for in such a creation the author does not communicate directly but through a kind of covering or disguise, fictitious persons or characters, who are more or less in evidence and who speak in his works. As T. S. Eliot remarks, poetry "is not the expression of personality, but an escape from personality." A literary work is a sign of special alienation, for wherever we have literary creation some sort of mask inevitably appears. In *The Sound and the Fury* Faulkner nowhere emerges as Faulkner in the way he does in his Nobel Prize speech. The bard who sings the ballad is not the same person who sits down to eat afterwards. The courier who brings news by word of mouth is. The orator, being partly creative, both is and is not the same.

In the case of the drama, the communication is still more complicated by another echelon of persons coming between the writer and his audience, the actors themselves. Actors are real persons, but they perform not as the persons they are, but as persons they are not. They have at times worn masks, to show that they are not themselves, but something other. And yet, is it not highly indicative that the word for mask, *persona* ("that through which the sound comes"), has given both to the ancients and to us the word for person? It is as though this ability to take on the role of another shows the actor's own humanity, shows that the other is already within him, and is, indeed, the shadow of his most real self. Ortega y Gasset points out that the brute animal is pure *alteración,* pure "otheration," in the sense that he cannot enter into himself. Man is not pure "otheration," because he can enter into himself—and yet, by the same token, he can find in himself and recognize by contrast the echoes of the personal other, the "thou," the alienation or *alteración* which is there. Thus acting a role, realizing in a specially intense way one's identity (in a sense) with a someone who (in another sense) one is not, remains one of the most human things a man can do. No brute animal can act a role. Unable to recognize himself, he finds it impossible to recognize what by contrast with self is other. By the same token, he has nothing against which to set a role so that it is a role.

II

Voice is the foundation for role-playing among men in the sense that the use of voice and its understanding, as we have seen, forces man to enter into others. From this point of view, it is not strange that as literature develops in the course of history, roles become more manifold and more complex. Homer's Odysseus plays a great many roles, but how many more are played, and played designedly, by the modern Ulysses, Leopold Bloom? And how many more, still, are played by the voice whom the reader hears—it does not matter here whether or not he knows that the work is by James Joyce—narrating the story *Ulysses?* Over and beyond all the other roles in which it is involved (those of Bloom and of all the other characters) is the voice playing the role of mocker, making fun of itself?

Whatever the answer, a role cannot exist outside a context of belief, and it is my purpose here to discuss how it is that, since voice demands role-playing, taking the part of the other within who is not ourselves, it demands belief as well, and how it is that belief is thus not something superadded to communication and thought, but something endemic to all human thinking, so that the question of belief and literature is really a specific variant of the general question concerning belief and communication in general, and ultimately concerning belief and human thought itself. All human intellectual activity implies belief because it implies faith in the possibility of communication and faith in someone with whom we can communicate.

Here one must make the well-known distinction between belief as opinion and belief as faith. Essentially, as Gabriel Marcel points out, belief as opinion is belief *that* and faces toward what it is concerned with as toward an object or "thing" or "fact" (a truth considered as a thing), as when I say, "I believe that tomorrow will be rainy," or "I believe that this book would sell well." Belief as faith, on the other hand, is belief *in* and faces toward a person or persons, as when I say, "I believe in Matthew," or "I believe in God." Belief as opinion is impersonal and should be impersonal, for its whole rationale is its "objectivity." Even if it is concerned with a person, it treats the person "objectively," not as someone to commune with but as an object to be measured. Thus, "I believe that Matthew is a competent reporter." Belief as faith, on the contrary, is personal in cast, and must be.

However, despite these contrasts between opinion and faith, it is no accident that the term "belief" is used for both, since opinion and faith are indissolubly related by the commerce they carry on with one another. Thus, although belief as faith basically is belief *in* a person, it is also possible to believe *in* a thing or an object by giving it a personalist cast. Thus, "I believe *in* this book" erects the book into more than an object. It makes of it a cause, with all the personal issues which this involves. It throws down the gauntlet on behalf of the author, whereas "I believe that this book would sell well" does not necessarily do so. Conversely, to believe *in* a person (belief as faith) involves a certain belief *that* what he says (in so far as he understands and controls it) is true.

Moreover, it appears that any belief *in* (belief as faith) not only is directed toward a person but also involves in one way or another his truthfulness, his "word." This is shown in part by the fact that one cannot believe in a liar as a pure liar (if such a man can exist). But something more profound than this negative example is involved. For belief in a person is ultimately an invitation to the person to respond. As Gabriel Marcel has pointed out in *The Mystery of Being,* belief in a person may include all sorts of beliefs *that,* varying from mere conjectural opinion (thus I believe that my friend will act considerately) to the acceptance of the truth of something of which I do not have direct knowledge (thus belief in God includes the acceptance of the existence of God as a truth, belief *that* God exists). But belief in a person includes also much more than this. To believe *in* God is to look for a response from Him. The construction of our expression and thinking with the term "in"—a construction found in many languages other than English—is significant here. It suggests that somehow in believing *in* someone, we enter into him. He is not merely an "object" of belief with whom our belief terminates. He is an interiority into whom our belief penetrates and with whom it enables us to commune. The expression suggests the same interpenetration of I and thou which, we have seen, underlies all human communication.

This brings home to us the fact that all communication—and, indeed, all our thinking, which is learned and developed only through communication with others—goes on in a context of belief. For when we speak, we invite response. If I expect no response, no "yes," or "no," no riposte of any sort, at least internal, I do not normally speak at all—unless I am losing hold on myself, am distraught, or am not in my right mind. Now, any expectation of response is in some way a declaration of belief in the person or persons to whom I address myself. It is recognition of a presence to whose word I can, in turn, attend, and in whom I can thus believe through the acceptance of what he has to say.

Since belief, either as opinion or as faith, includes some sort of acceptance or commitment without full "objective" evidence, belief as faith, or belief *in,* surpasses belief as opinion, or belief *that.* Belief as opinion moves toward knowledge of objects, but, since it has not sufficient contact with objects to amount to full knowledge, it is essentially deficient and vulnerable. Belief as faith moves toward knowledge and love of persons, and since persons cannot be known as objects at all, no matter how intimately they are seized, the lack of "objective" evidence here is not the liability that it is in the case of belief as opinion.

This situation can be restated in terms of the way in which belief as opinion and belief as faith differ with regard to their relationship to words. Belief as opinion tends to do away with words in so far as it is ordered to "objective" knowledge, which has to do with things which do not speak. Belief as faith, on the other hand, since it has to do with persons, tends not to eliminate words but rather dwells in words and feeds on them, since they are manifestations of persons. Further, in so far as communication with persons is better, more human, and, we might add, holier than contact with objects, belief as faith outclasses belief as opinion. Opinion is styled belief because it can be thought of as analogous to belief as faith. But belief as faith is simply belief in its purest form. For, short of direct observation, the best contact we can have with objects and facts is not opinions about them gleaned from imperfect evidence but faith regarding them —that is, knowledge derived from our acceptance of the word of other persons who have this knowledge by direct observation.

Of the knowledge which individual men have today, almost all is grounded in faith. The knowledge of scientists themselves is almost all grounded in faith, well-founded and rational faith in the reports of their fellow-scientists, but faith nevertheless. Of the scientific knowledge which any man has, only a tiny fraction has been achieved by his own direct observation. For the rest, he has good reason to believe *that* it is true because, within the limits of their competence, he believes *in* his fellow-scientists reporting on their work or reporting reports of the work of others. Thus, even in the most "objective" of fields, in actuality the word of persons is more pervasive than factual observation. Science itself cannot live save in a network of belief. Even in science, where fact is more determinative, presence is nevertheless more pervasive than fact.

III

Against this background, the question of belief in literature can be raised. A survey of current writing in English on this question shows that it is pretty well all concerned with literature as involving belief *that*. The grounds of the question are staked out in terms of Coleridge's "willing suspension of disbelief," so that the problem becomes, as in Richards's *Practical Criticism,* how can one who does not share Donne's Christian faith enter into his sonnet *At the Round Earth's Imagined Corners Blow?* Or, to adapt Richards's terminology, how can one share Donne's beliefs emotionally while not sharing them intellectually?

This focus of the question of belief in literature is legitimate. However, we must remember that it considers belief as concerned with a kind of object or "thing," excised from any personal context. The notion of response to a presence, manifested by voice, drops out entirely, although such response seems intimately a part of literature. Objects cannot elicit response to a voice in the way in which persons can, and when we treat belief in terms of the object of belief exclusively, response becomes attenuated to behavior, and its correlative is not voice but stimulus in the Pavlovian pattern of stimulus-response. It is significant that Professor Richards not only concerns himself with "willing suspension of disbelief" but also, perhaps not entirely out of line with Coleridge's thinking even here, regularly discusses literature in terms of the way words "behave," as though words were not cries but "things," visible objects. We have a right, of course, to speak of words in terms of this analogy, but let us not forget that it is an analogy.

Without attempting to deal with the question of belief on these grounds, which are perhaps closer to Mr. Abrams's concerns than to mine here, I should like to set it up on other grounds and to examine it there, not with a view to providing utterly conclusive answers but to improve our perspectives and to reveal how limited some of our common views of this problem really are. Let us recall that in the last analysis, any utterance, even a scientific utterance, is the manifestation of a presence, which cannot be "grasped" as an "object" of knowledge can be, but only invoked or evoked. The most abstruse mathematical theorem remains always and inextricably within this framework of utterance, for it originated as something communicable and remains always something which someone *says* to others or, in special cases, to himself. But, since in the case of scientific utterance the vocal element is minimized, we can treat such utterance readily as an object and speak with ease of "grasping" or "not grasping" it, as we might an object. Thus, we grasp or we do not grasp the meaning of the formula $E=mc^2$. But we know how difficult and unconvincing it is to apply the notion of "grasp" to a poetic work. The notion can, of course, be applied to some extent. We can speak of "grasping" *Hamlet* or *The Marriage of Heaven and Hell* or *Absalom, Absalom!* But so to speak is not very satisfactory, not convincing. It seems much more real to speak of the response which these works evoke from us. The "evocative" quality—which is to say, the "calling" quality—is paramount in a work of real literature. Literature exists in a context of one presence calling to another.

This is a context of faith, no matter how much there may be in an individual work which, outside the work, we can know by direct evidence. Indeed, here faith achieves a special intensity (and simultaneously a special attenuation) in so far as the voice which invokes us as present and evokes our response is in a way more a pure or self-subsistent voice because of the "objective" quality of the literary work as such, its detachment from the poet, who, as an individual, is dissociated from the work by his literary mask. There is a special kind of dialectic at work here. In so far as the work is objectified, set apart from the existent writer who gives it being as a kind of well-wrought urn is detached from its creator, its evocative effect becomes more poignant. Thus Yeats went to Japanese Nō plays for "more formal faces," explaining that "a mask [even taken metaphorically] . . . no matter how close you go is still a work of art." Joyce's progress from *Stephen Hero* through *A Portrait of the Artist* to *Ulysses* and *Finnegans Wake* is progress from personal involvement to artistic detachment, and, as the mask-like detachment grows, the evocative quality of the work, its pull on the sensibilities of the reader, grows. Because Poe can never achieve so great a detachment, because his personal problems and neuroses show through —to those, at any rate, for whom Poe's English is their native language, as it was not for Baudelaire and Mallarmé—the evocative quality of his work remains less poignant than that of Joyce or, to take another American, that of Faulkner.

We might ask why this is. If voice is an invitation to response, in what sense can the invitation become more insistent when the speaker wears a mask? To see what is involved in this question, one must consider the peculiar conditions of person-to-person communication, which is implemented by the use of voice. Human persons are of themselves distant from one another in the sense that they cannot enter entirely into one another's consciousness. The sense of distance attending on personal or I-thou relationships has been elaborated by recent writers such as Lavelle, Heidegger, and Buber, but once it is stated it needs no great explanation, for we live with this sense all the time. In dealing with another person, I am always dealing with one whom I cannot entirely fathom and with whom I cannot enter into direct communication quite like the communication I enter into with myself. His sense of self remains outside my direct awareness, and yet I can feel its aura and know that there is some interiority with whom I am dealing.

My contact with this interiority is mediated by exterior phenomena which implement commerce between interiors. This commerce is most readily maintained by voice. Voice is the least exterior of sensible phenomena because it emanates not only from the physical but also from the divided psychological interior of man and penetrates to another physical and psychological interior where, as we have seen, it must be recreated in the imagination in order to live. Unlike a picture, it lives by its contact with these interiors—when they are gone, it is gone.

Still, for all this interior orientation, even a voice is an exterior something. It achieves its effect through an exterior medium. Our way of harkening to one another, and thus our sense of presence, necessitates a kind of break-through. We penetrate into a "thou" through a something which is neither "I" nor "thou," through a medium over which the action emanating from one person exercises an effect on another. Even direct physical contact involves an externalizing medium, for our body is, in a sense, not so much our self as our consciousness is. Even in its interior, our body is somehow the "outside" of us.

The exteriority attendant on communication is what gives point to the mask in dramatic performance and, analogically, in all literature. Although it modifies the presence which manifests itself most poignantly in voice, of itself the mask is not vocal, but a medium manifest in space. It does not modify the voice of the character (presence, person) as the mute modifies the sound on a violin. Even though masks may occasionally affect voice projection, to do so is not the mask's primary function, for it is patently objectified as a visual phenomenon and produces its characteristic effects by being seen. It stands for that in the person-to-person situation which is nonvocal, noncommunicative, nonpersonal, remote, alienated.

In the preliterate world, where the eye is especially subservient to the ear, masks themselves are felt as belonging rather more to the world of voice than they are today, or perhaps are caught up more thoroughly into the world of voice, and esthetic distance tends to disappear. For the Wintu, Dorothy Lee has noted, Coyote, Buzzard, and Grizzly Bear are bewilderingly man and animal. Although the wearer of a wolf mask among primitives is not a wolf, he somehow really participates in wolfness. In this situation, where the object-world is not clearly differentiated from the world of voice and person, belief has not the depth of meaning it enjoys in a civilized society, for the same reason that science itself has not: the two are confounded with one another, for the dialectic which sets them apart with some precision has not yet sufficiently progressed.

This seems to have been the state of affairs with the very early Greeks in their ritualistic use of masks. Later, with the great tragedians, real characters appear, and the masks worn become devices establishing esthetic distance, *alteración,* limited more definitely to the universe of space. For space separates, whereas voice unites. As this evolution takes place, the number and complexities of roles, and of literary forms, proliferate. The means of controlling and differentiating characters and forms have been developed as the tension between the vocal and the visual grows. For this tension the mask is the symbol, or in a later day costume and makeup, a mitigated form of mask.

As the tension between visual and vocal grows, and with it the use of the truly dramatic character and the formalized separation of drama from life, there grows also, paradoxically, an awareness of the foundation in real human existence for dramatic character. A character in a drama is a person set off, advertised as other. Yet this state of being set off, this remoteness in the midst of intimacy, is found in real life, too, and experience of drama teaches us to recognize the fact. Each man is always in some degree a mask to other men, more consciously so today because of the progressive reflectiveness which mankind develops in its passage through history.

The sense of being set off is not annihilated by intimacy. Indeed, it is heightened and realized in its fullness through intimacy because of the very interiority which makes possible

intimacy between persons. As a unique and induplicable individual abiding in the depths of your own interior consciousness, you are in a way more other to me than even inanimate objects are. And this despite the fact that I can carry on a dialogue with you and cannot carry on a dialogue with inanimate objects. For in assuring me of my closeness to your consciousness, this dialogue assures me also of the uniqueness of your consciousness and of its ultimate inviolability—of the fact that, naturally speaking, I can never know what it is to be you, can never share this ultimate experience of yourself with you. Of course, I cannot know what it is to be an object either—a rosebush or a canary—but neither can the object know what it is to be itself, so that this lack of knowledge on my part does not prevent a quite full knowledge of the object. Object-being includes no experience of self to be shared. What uniqueness the object has is imputed to it from the outside. In the case of a person, however, his experience of his unique self is constitutive of his most intimate self. And yet it is this very experience that intimacy cannot share.

IV

These considerations throw some light on what happens to the personal charge carried by a voice in the case of a work of literature—of poetry, let us say, to take a relatively pure instance of literature. In a poem, the voice is there, but "objectified" in such a way as to mask the real person who uttered it in the first place and any other real person who utters it after him. A poem thus advertises the distance and remoteness which, paradoxically, is part of every human attempt to communicate, and it does this in so far as it is under one aspect "objective," an "objective correlative," object-like, which is to say nonvocal. But under a certain aspect only, for under another it is not object-like, since it is indeed attempting to communicate.

Given the effective drive toward communication, the more the remoteness between the voice which, working within this drive, really creates the poem (that is, the voice of the writer) and those who hear or read it, the more evocative the work becomes. The drama is the most evocative and personal of all literary forms. In it living persons on a real stage really speak to one another. And yet, here the remoteness between point of origin and point of assimilation has actually been increased because the number of masks has been increased: in a performance of *Othello,* besides the mask or masks which Shakespeare as author wears, there is the mask of a character which each performer wears and which makes him precisely a *dramatis persona,* a person or mask in the drama. The reason for the corresponding heightening of effect seems to be the fact that all communication takes place across barriers, or is an attempt to crash through barriers, namely, the barriers which bar the ultimate compenetration of the "I" and the "thou." Provided that communication is going on, the interposition of further barriers has a tantalizing effect. It teases us to more vigorous attempts, sharper alertness, greater efforts at compassion or sympathy. One thinks of the poignancy achieved by the device of the wall in the story of Pyramus and Thisbe.

But certain other parallels might be adduced to show the intensification of the personal charge by the interposition of a mask or other barrier. A major one is in the religious history of

Judaism and Christianity, where, moreover, the connection becomes evident between person and mask on the one hand and faith on the other. Compared with Aristotle, who thought it impossible that God should concern Himself at all with human affairs, Hebrews and Christians know God in a highly personal fashion. And yet they know Him by faith, which is in a kind of mask, "through a glass darkly." Moreover, in the Christian dispensation God reveals Himself more personally to man when the Second Person of the Trinity, Whose personal name is the Word as well as the Son, takes to Himself a human nature which masks His divinity. His Passion, where His human nature is seen through the mask of death, is memorialized in the Eucharist, where the human and divine natures of the Word are both masked under the appearances of bread and wine, which also, by symbolic separation of His Body and Blood, masks His human death itself. But this "masking" only heightens the personal relationship between God and man, for through the Eucharist the personal union of Christians in the Person of Christ and thence in the other two Persons of the Godhead is realized and perpetuated. Although not applied to what we are discussing here, this sense of the Eucharist is highly operative in Christian tradition. It accounts for a favorite name of the Eucharist, Holy Communion, that is, Holy Togetherness. Its implications are elaborated by St. Thomas Aquinas and other theologians, who point out, moreover, that the consecration of the elements in this sacrament of sacraments is effected not by any sign in space, but by *words* given us by the Word of God. The whole setting for this series of masks is one of communication of

the most personal sort, in a universe of words and of faith,
where sight is at one or more removes from full reality.

v

The masks in literature are generally assumed by one party
to communication rather than by both. The playwright and the
actors, who are the communicators, assume the masks—the playwright a metaphorical one and the actors real ones or their
equivalent in costume and makeup. By contrast, the hearer is
present in his own person. Were he to put on a mask, he would
become a part of the play, a *dramatis persona*. As it is, although
the actors and the play may enrapture him, carry him somewhat
out of himself, they do not make him into a quasi-other person.
The act on his part which corresponds to the masking on the
part of the communicators is simply his act of belief, in the
sense of faith. And belief here is not at all tantamount to opinion.
One has no "opinion" that Sir Laurence Olivier is Hamlet, and
no "opinion" that Ophelia's death is real. Belief *that* is relatively
meaningless here. This belief is more radically belief *in,* and such
belief is not pretended.

But belief in whom? In whoever are the persons behind the
masks. In the actors and the playwright all together. The act
of faith, or belief *in* is an invitation to them to respond as persons, to give themselves in and through truth. And, while there
is also a certain faith in the audience which playwright and
actors both have, a belief *in* the audience, an invitation to the
audience to respond—for this faith, as we have seen, accom-
panies all human communication—nevertheless this faith of the

playwright and the actors is less obviously faith than that of the audience. The reason is the curious one-way nature of artistic communication, the fact that no real dialogue takes place, that the audience itself has no occasion or opportunity to speak. The audience's response is hidden, as the act of faith on the part of the playwright and actors is correspondingly hidden. The response of the playwright and actors, on the other hand, to the audience's faith is the play itself, which is far from hidden since the audience's act of faith is quite obvious.

In response to the audience's act of faith the playwright and the actors give themselves in and through truth. How the truth is contained in the words of the play—or, *mutatis mutandis,* in the poem or other piece of literature—and, indeed, what the truth in question really is, may be a very mysterious matter. This is to be expected. The truths arrived at by faith, natural as well as supernatural, are not noted for readily admitting of clear-cut statement or of clear-cut assimilation nor for being entirely evident to everyone, even to those of good will. They often submit reluctantly or not at all to full articulation, for they have to do most intimately with persons to whom we address ourselves. If they are neatly articulated, they are taken not on their own evidence but on the evidence of a person to whom we address our act of faith. And it is hard to articulate a person. For a person whom we are addressing nature provides us no distinctive word while we are addressing him save the strange noun-substitute or name-substitute or pro-noun "thou," which is not a name at all but changes its entire meaning with each different person we apply it to.

Our belief in a play or a poem is thus an invitation to the

persons involved in composing it and presenting it to us either
to say something worth our while or to betray our trust in them
as persons. It involves a kind of openness to them and to their
meaning at all levels, to what Professor Philip Wheelwright in
The Burning Fountain styles "depth experience." If certain details of a poem seem unacceptable to us in terms of belief *that,*
the voice of the poem, coming through the mask of its speaker
(as well as through the masks of any characters he may have
introduced) teases us on, so that beneath any disagreement with
detail there persists the conviction that something worthy of
assent is being said, into which the otherwise unacceptable detail may somehow be fitted. If we cannot believe in Prospero as
a real magician, we can believe that the playwright is using him
to convey some further word or truth to us.

In *La parole et l'écriture* Louis Lavelle makes much of the
"world" as language. For communication to be possible there
must be a world shared by our individual consciences so that
by naming the objects in this world we can break through our
solitude and communicate with one another. When a child believes that he knows something as soon as he can name it, he is
not entirely wrong. For when he can name it, he can use it for
what it is worth, as a means of communicating with others. That
which is neither you nor I, once it is known, becomes a link
uniting you and me. This is true not only of the natural world
which we apprehend through our senses, but also of poetry and
of literature in general. Poetry is often involved and mysterious,
but by its very existence within our ken it is destined to communicate. Indeed, its communication is in one sense communication *par excellence,* the most intimate communication. John

Stuart Mill's notion, romantically rooted, that poetry is something which is overheard is a not too happy attempt to deal with the intimacy which poetry can effect: so intimate is the union of hearer and poet that it is as though the hearer as other were not there. The opinion sometimes expressed that poetry or art in general is basically not communicative at all is connected with this dialectical situation in which estrangement (the mask of the poet) and intimacy (achieved when the mask is somehow penetrated) are so strangely compounded.

If a poem is likened to an object in the world, it must be likened to an object already named, converted for purposes of communication, if named with a quite mysterious name. "Poetic truth," which seems so difficult to bring to earth, to isolate, to state clearly, and which is also so strangely intimate, has its roots in a sense of communion with other persons, persons perceived through masks, yet somehow decidedly there, who have believed in us enough to invite us to this uncommonly intimate response and in whom we, in turn, are called on to believe.

We come to the conclusion that any belief *that* involved in literature is subservient to belief *in,* that the most basic meaning of belief in literature has to do not with belief in the sense of opinion, which regards objects and facts (truths treated as objects), but with belief in the sense of faith, which regards person-to-person relationships, invitations and response, and truth with reference to these relationships. This conclusion is, I believe, nowhere more strikingly evident than in the situation which has obtained for some years in twentieth-century poetry. The withdrawal of the serious poet (or of the serious artist generally) has been commented on *ad nauseam*. Withdrawal from what or into what? Into himself, we are told. Yet we are faced with the striking fact that serious readers of poetry today favor no other type of poetry so much as this poetry of withdrawal. The conclusion would seem to be that readers like nothing better than to follow the poet into his retreat. Everybody wants to be alone together. And this is not strange. There is no doubt that in our age, which has evolved, among other things, a mass culture and mass media of communication, intimacy is also in many ways better served than it has ever been before. Certainly the human race is more conscious of itself as a whole and has developed its dialogue about intimacy and communication more than at earlier periods in human history. We have a more highly perfected vocabulary and more advanced means of articulation about this subject than ever before. However aware earlier man may have been of persons and of the "I-thou" situation, the philosophy known as personalism is a twentieth-century creation, just as thoroughly a product of our age as technology or television commercials. In this climate belief *in* becomes very meaningful. In terms of belief as we have viewed it here, the serious modern reader wants to believe in his poets more than ever before. This would seem to indicate that in the age of television voice is in some ways regaining a prestige over sight, that we are at the end of the Gutenberg era.

The Collaboration of Vision in the Poetic Act: The Religious Dimension

Rhythm and ideation, song and vision, collaborate in the poetic act. . . .

—Philip Wheelwright

Vision is perhaps the poet's morality.

—Wallace Fowlie

Since it is the assigned task of this essay to deal with the religious "periphery" of literary art, it seems incumbent upon me to observe at the outset that this notion that the issues of religion are peripheral to the main issues that face the student of literature may itself reflect a situation of crisis in contemporary criticism. The crisis that I have in mind is one that arises out of what is central and decisive in the doctrines of modern poetics, and it is a crisis that was given a kind of desperate announcement a few years ago when Allen Tate bluntly raised the question which it is a peculiarity of our generation to be anxious about— namely, "is literary criticism possible?" [1]

---

[1] The reference is to Mr. Tate's essay "Is Literary Criticism Possible?" in *The Forlorn Demon* (Chicago, 1953).

It would not, of course, at first appear that the man of letters in our time feels himself to be at such an extremity, for one of the patron saints of the modern movement has assured us that the contemporary critic is "among the most presentable instances of modern man" and that in depth and precision his work is "beyond all earlier criticism in our language." And on all sides today we are frequently given similar testimonies of how unparalleled in any previous age are the vigor and trenchancy of criticism in our own time. So, with a zeal that is itself certainly unparalleled in any previous time, the contemporary achievement is anthologized almost annually; and the editors of the journals in which it has gained expression frequently engage their colleagues in symposia the aim of which is to indicate the gains that have been made and the solid ground on which we may now take our stand. But in all this stocktaking I think we may sense a certain anxious uncertainty as to whether anything has been achieved at all and as to whether, in the presence of the great works of the past and of the modern period, we are yet able really to penetrate the ontological intransigeance of the aesthetic fact. And it is just possible that, despite the actual impressiveness of the achievement of modern criticism, this anxiety is a consequence of the doctrine which it has promoted and which has had the ironical effect of calling into question the very possibility of criticism itself. Indeed, what I want to propose is that, if we will take thought again of the first principles by which we have undertaken in our time to reckon with the reality of literary art, we may be put in mind not only of what in part our present distresses in criticism derive from but also of what is problematic in our understanding of the religious dimensions of imaginative literature.

Now when we seek for the principal motives that underlie the general movement of criticism in our period, we cannot for long escape the recognition that, among them at least, has been the intention of many of its most distinguished representatives to offer some resistance to the reductionist tendency of modern scientism, particularly when it broaches upon those transactions with reality that are peculiar to the humanistic imagination. I can think of no single doctrine or emphasis that is subscribed to by all those writers who at one time or another have been held accountable for "the new criticism," but certainly by far a greater number of them are of a single mind in their apprehensiveness about the deeper cultural implications of the reigning positivism than they are on any other single point. And it has been their unwillingness to give their suffrage to the absolute hegemony of empirical science which has been a decisive influence upon their approach to the fundamental issues in theory of literature. Ours has, of course, been a time in which it has been generally supposed that the only responsible versions of experience that can be had are those afforded us by the empirical sciences and in which, therefore, the common impulse has been to trivialize the arts by regarding them, in Arthur Mizener's phrase, as a kind of "amiable insanity" which, at best, is to be tolerated for the sedative effect that it has upon the nervous system. But even this assignment hardly constitutes a satisfactory charter for the artist, since, in the ministry of health to the nervous system, he is not likely to compete successfully with our modern doctors of psychology. So, in the last analysis, our culture has been incapable of finding for the arts, and especially for literature, a valuable or an irreplaceable function. And the result has been that the major

strategists of modern criticism have felt it incumbent upon themselves to revindicate the poetic enterprise by doing what the culture was unable to do—namely, by seeking to define that unique
and indispensable role in the human economy that is played by
imaginative literature and that can be preempted by nothing else.

This contemporary effort to specify the nature of the autonomy
which a work of literary art possesses has, of course, involved a
careful analysis of what is special in the linguistic strategies of
the poet. And the aim has been to establish that poetry is poetry
and not another thing, for it has been recognized that in a culture as dominated by scientific procedure as is our own the common tendency is to hold all forms of discourse accountable to
those critical canons that are really appropriate only to scientific
modes of discourse—which, of course, then makes it possible for
nonscientific modes of statement to be quickly dismissed on one
pretext or another. So the tack that the contemporary movement
in criticism has taken has been one that involves the denial that
the poet is any sort of expositor at all. He is, we have been told,
not an expositor, not a Platonist, not an allegorist, not a merchant
in the business of ideas: on the contrary, he is a certain kind of
technician, a certain kind of maker, who constructs out of language special sorts of things, such things as we call dramas and
novels and poems. And, as the doctrine runs, what is distinctive
about the language of imaginative literature is that, in contrast to
the ordinary forms of expository discourse, it does not involve
the reduction of words to the level of being merely conceptual
signs. That is to say, it does not lead us beyond itself into some
external realm of meaning; it is, rather, a language that is so
thoroughly composed and that is so heavily charged with imag-

inative intensity that, unlike other forms of discourse, it is capable of capturing attention *intransitively* upon itself.[2] It is, indeed, the one form of discourse that, in its operations, manages to avoid any bifurcation between the thing or event and the words which refer to it. The language of poetry does not convey any rhetorical propositions about the issues of religion or politics or psychology or science; that is to say, it does not conduct the mind beyond itself to anything at all but rather leads us deeper and deeper into itself, in a process of exploration.

Our immunity from any compulsion to relate the language of the poem to an external reality has, in recent criticism, been understood in terms of the organic character of poetic structure. Which is to say that the contemporary critic has come to see poetic meaning not as a function of the relationships between the terms of the poem and some reality which is extrinsic to them but rather as a function of the interrelationships that knit the terms together into the total pattern that forms the unity of the work. Our way of stating this distinctive character of poetic language is to say that its terms function not ostensively but reflexively, not semantically but syntactically—by which we mean that, unlike the situation that obtains in logical discourse in which the terms "retain their distinctive characters despite the relationship into which they have been brought," [3] in poetic discourse they lose their distinctive characters, as they fuse into

[2] See Eliseo Vivas, "A Definition of the Aesthetic Experience," in *The Problems of Aesthetics,* ed. by Eliseo Vivas and Murray Krieger (New York, 1953), pp. 406–11. It is to Mr. Vivas that we are indebted for the definition in contemporary aesthetics of the poetic experience in terms of "intransitive attention." This concept receives further elaboration in his book *Creation and Discovery* (New York, 1955).

[3] Ernst Cassirer, *Language and Myth,* trans. by Susanne K. Langer (New York, 1946), p. 91.

one another and are modified by what Cleanth Brooks calls "the
pressure of the context." [4] It is, indeed, this whole phenomenon
to which Brooks has appropriately applied the term *irony,* a concept that he has insisted upon by way of emphatically remarking
the radical extent to which the terms and "statements" of a literary work bear the pressure of the total context and have their
meanings modified by that context. And it will be remembered
that in a brilliant passage in *The Well Wrought Urn* he suggests
that they ought even to be read as if they were speeches in a
drama, since, as he says, if they are to be justified at all, it will
not be by virtue of their "scientific or historical or philosophical
truth, but [they will, rather, be] justified in terms of a principle
analogous to that of dramatic propriety." [5]

Now it is in terms of this organic character of poetic structure
that our generation has come to understand the resistance of literary art to the discursive paraphrase. It does not yield a series of
paraphrasable abstractions because no set of terms of which a
poetic work is constituted refers to anything extrinsic to the
work: they refer, rather, to the other terms to which they are
related within the work. And thus the perception of the meaning
of the work awaits not an act of comparison between the com-
ponent terms and the external objects or events which they may
be taken to symbolize but awaits, rather, an act of imaginative
prehension that will focus upon "the entire pattern of internal
reference . . . apprehended as a unity." [6] The coherence of a

[4] "Irony as a Principle of Structure," *Literary Opinion in America,* ed. by
Morton Dauwen Zabel (New York, 1951), pp. 730–31.
[5] *The Well Wrought Urn* (London, 1949), p. 188.
[6] Joseph Frank, "Spatial Form in Modern Literature," *Criticism: The Founda-
tions of Modern Literary Judgment,* ed. by Mark Schorer *et al* (New York, 1948),
p. 383. Mr. Frank's essay contains some very acute observations upon the "re-
flexive" character of poetic language.

work of imaginative literature is to be sought, in other words, not in any set of logically manageable propositions into which it may be paraphrased but rather in the living pattern of inter-related themes and "resolved stresses" [7] that the work contains.

There is, however, one inescapable fact that such a formulation of poetic meaning may at first appear to neglect, and it is the incorrigibly referential thrust that words do have. They like to function "ostensively": that is to say, they insist upon pointing to things: it makes no difference whether the things are actual or ideal: what counts is that they are extrinsic to the words themselves, for the words are not happy unless they are performing a semantic function. And, this being their habit, it would seem that they would be intractable by the poetic purpose. But this problem is recognized by contemporary theorists who, indeed, have come to regard the poetic labor as involving in part an effort to deliver the word from its ordinary logical bonds and its inherent mediateness. As Ezra Pound once remarked, the poet "takes words ordinarily having conventional objective meanings, and by forcing them into a new and independent structure objectifies fresh meanings. . . . The function of the artist," said Pound, "is precisely the formulation of what has not found its way into language, i.e. any language, verbal, plastic or musical." [8] And it is precisely this effort of the poet to perform not simply an act of denotation but the far more difficult act of evocation, of capturing and conveying the full, living body of the world and of objectifying fresh experience of it—it is precisely this effort

[7] Brooks, *The Well Wrought Urn*, p. 186.

[8] "Epstein, Belgion and Meaning," *The Criterion*, Vol. IX, No. XXXVI (April, 1930), p. 471.

that very often commits him to the daring project of liberating words from the logical form into which they conventionally fall, so that they may be free to enter into the characteristic structures of poetic form in which they are affected by, and in turn affect, the total context established by the work. This is why you do not discover the meaning of a poem by taking an inventory of the various terms of which it is constituted and then by adding up the various meanings which these terms have in conventional usage. And when contemporary criticism insists upon the foolishness of such a procedure, it does so because it is sensitive, perhaps above all else, to the marvelous violence of the action that is performed upon terms once they are drawn up into the poetic process, so that each alters under the aspect of the other and enters relationships that are completely irreducible to logical form and gathers a quite new meaning from the role that it assumes in the total configuration. It is the mystery that T. S. Eliot had in mind when he remarked upon "that perpetual slight alteration of language, words perpetually juxtaposed in new and sudden combination," which takes place in poetry.

So we may say, then, by way of summary, that the redefinition in our time of the nature of literary art has led to the view that the given work exists in and through its language. What we have immediately before us is a patterned mosaic in language which is, in the phrase by which Denis de Rougemont speaks of the work of art in general, "a calculated trap for meditation" [9]—and as such it effectively insists that before it we perform an act of rapt and "intransitive attention." One might even say that for the modern sensibility the poetry in the poem resides "not [in]

---

[9] "Religion and the Mission of the Artist," in *Spiritual Problems in Contemporary Literature,* ed. by Stanley R. Hopper (New York, 1952), p. 177.

some intrinsic quality (beauty or truth) of the materials" [10] with which the poet builds his poem but resides rather in the completeness of the unity or "composition" that he contrives out of the stuff of language. What we begin with, as Eliot has told us, is simply "excellent words in excellent arrangement." [11]

Now this redefinition in modern criticism of "the mode of existence of a literary work of art" has in turn led to a redefinition of the creative process. For so rigorous has been the stress that has been put upon the autonomy of poetic language that language itself has often very nearly been regarded as the enabling cause of literary art. It is assumed that art is a virtue of the practical intellect and that the poet's vision is not fully formed until it has been objectified in language. Indeed, the executive principle of the creative process is considered really to derive not from the poet's metaphysic or his special perspective upon the human story but rather from the medium to which his vision is submitted and by which it is controlled. It is regarded as a truism that whatever it is that the poet "says" about reality in a given work is something the content of which he was not himself in possession of until the completion of the work. For, as Murray Krieger has recently put it, "the poet's original idea for his work, no matter how clearly thought out and complete he thinks it is, undergoes such radical transformations as language goes creatively to work upon it that the finished poem, in its full internal relations, is far removed from what the author thought he had when he began." [12] The medium alone, in other

[10] Cleanth Brooks, *Modern Poetry and the Tradition* (Chapel Hill, N. C., 1939), p. 43.

[11] T. S. Eliot, Preface to the 1928 edition of *The Sacred Wood* (London, 1934, 4th ed.), pp. ix–x.

[12] *The New Apologists for Poetry* (Minneapolis, 1956), p. 23.

words, objectifies the poet's materials and gives them their implications. This axiom of the contemporary movement in criticism is expressed with especial directness by R. P. Blackmur, when he remarks in his essay on Melville:

> Words, and their intimate arrangements, must be the ultimate as well as the immediate source of every effect in the written or spoken arts. Words bring meaning to birth and themselves contained the meaning as an imminent possibility before the pangs of junction. To the individual artist the use of words is an adventure in discovery; the imagination is heuristic among the words it manipulates. The reality you labour desperately or luckily to put into your words . . . you will actually have found there, deeply ready and innately formed to give an objective being and specific idiom to what you knew and did not know that you knew.[13]

Whatever it is, in other words, that is in the completed work is there by virtue of the language which controls the creative process and which produces the "new word" that Yvor Winters declares the authentic work of literary art to be. The poet does not have a version of the human situation to express, some imperious preoccupation to voice, or some difficult report to make: no, he has none of this: indeed, as Eliot tells us, there is no good reason for supposing that he does "any thinking on his own" at all, for it is not his business to think—not even poets as great as Dante and Shakespeare. No, all the writer need have is his medium, and, if he knows how to trust it and how to submit to it,

---

[13] "The Craft of Herman Melville: A Putative Statement," in *The Lion and the Honeycomb* (New York; 1955), p. 138.

it will do his work for him: it will, as Blackmur says, bring the "meaning to birth."

Now, to be sure, what I have offered thus far is patently an abridgment of the advanced poetics of our time, but perhaps this account is at least sufficiently complex to provide some indication of the sources of the crisis that I earlier remarked as having arisen in contemporary criticism. It is clear certainly that we are being asked by many of the most distinguished theorists of our day to regard the work of literary art as a linguistic artifact that exists in complete detachment from any other independently existent reality. The fully achieved work of art, as the argument runs, is a discrete and closed system of mutually interrelated terms: the organic character of the structure prevents the constituent terms from being atomistically wrenched out of their context and made to perform a simple referential function, and it also succeeds in so segregating the total structure from the circumambient world as to prevent its entering into any extramural affiliation. "A poem should not mean but be," says Archibald MacLeish, and thereby, in this famous line from his poem *Ars Poetica,* he summarizes, with a beautiful concision, the mind of a generation.

But then, of course, if the work of literary art exists in complete isolation from all those contexts that lie beyond the one established by the work itself, if it neither points outward toward the world nor inward toward the poet's subjectivity, if it is wholly self-contained and cut off from the general world of meaning, why, then it would seem that nothing really can be said about it at all. And in this unpromising strait are we not all chargeable with "the heresy of paraphrase"? Mark Van Doren suggests in his book *The Noble Voice* that "Any great poet is in a sense beyond criticism for the simple reason that he has written a successful story," that "Criticism is most at home with failure," and that in the presence of the great success it must be "as dumb as the least instructed reader." [14] This is, of course, hardly an inspiriting conclusion for the practicing critic to reach; yet it is, in a way, the conclusion that has been enforced upon him by the new poetics of our period. For the curious irony that has arisen out of the contemporary movement in criticism is a result of the fact that, on the one hand, it has striven for a concept of literary art that would permit responsible discussion of it as art rather than as something else but, on the other hand, it has succeeded in so completely segregating art from everything else that, in its presence, it has condemned itself, at least in principle, to silence. And this is, I believe, the reason for the noticeable anxiety in the critical forums today about whether anything has really been achieved at all. Much has been achieved, of course, in the establishment of a fund of substantiated judgments about literary texts, but the point is that this achievement has had no sanction in the body of principle to which our generation has come to subscribe, for that body of doctrine has tended ultimately to represent the aesthetic fact as unavailable for critical discussion. And thus it should perhaps, after all, not be surprising that the same distinguished critic who some years ago told us that the contempoary achievement surpassed "all earlier criticism in our language" is, in a more recent essay, to be found wondering why it is that critics don't

[14] *The Noble Voice* (New York, 1946), pp. 181–82.

go mad; and one of his equally distinguished friends often ruminates upon the "burden" that he and his colleagues in criticism today must bear.

The distresses and distempers that lead our most sensitive practical critics today to reflect upon the inhumanly difficult nature of their labors are, in other words, a result of their betrayal by the inadequate concept of literature that has descended to them from the main strategists in modern theory. There are many points at which this concept might now be put under some pressure, but that upon which I want to focus on this present occasion is the understanding of the creative process that has been promoted in our time, for here, I think, we may get as good a purchase as any other upon our present dilemmas. And when this aspect of modern theory is examined it becomes evident to how great a degree its legislation about the nature of the poetic object has determined its understanding of the process by which that object is made. What it has wanted to insist upon is the indissoluble unity of form and content in the work which gives it the kind of autonomy that prevents its being translated into any other mode of statement. And this concern has in turn led contemporary theorists to minimize the controlling effect upon the creative process of the writer's ideas and beliefs. For it has been supposed that, were any great tribute to be paid to these factors, we should be quickly on the way towards reinstating the heresy of didacticism, with its notion that the literary work is merely a rhetorical communication of independently formulable ideas. So great stress has been put upon the directive role of the medium in the creative process, and we have been reminded of how radical must be the transformations of the poet's ideas, once these ideas undergo the modifications necessitated by the exigencies of a developing linguistic structure. What we are asked to understand is that nothing really exists in imaginative literature, except as it is organized by the medium which is language. Indeed, whatever does exist is itself created by the language, for, as I. A. Richards says, it is the "means of that growth which is the mind's endless endeavour to order itself" [15]—or, as Blackmur expresses it in the passage which was quoted earlier, "Words bring meaning to birth and themselves contained the meaning as an imminent possibility before the pangs of junction." The medium, in other words, is a kind of intelligent agency which in some mysterious way puppetizes the poet and does the job for which, in its innocence, common sense has traditionally held him responsible.

I am aware, of course, that at this point I am to some extent exaggerating the contemporary testimony, but its own exaggerations in this matter are, I think, sufficiently great to make my characterization intelligible. In any event I am reassured by the coincidence that I discover between my own reaction and that of the English critic D. S. Savage, who suggests in the preface to his book *The Withered Branch* that this "dizzy elevation" of the medium in contemporary criticism clearly leaves something important out of account.[16] And there is, I believe, no finer recent statement of what is unaccounted for than that which Jacques Maritain gives us in his great book *Creative Intuition in Art and Poetry*.[17]

[15] *The Philosophy of Rhetoric* (New York, 1936), p. 131.

[16] *The Withered Branch* (New York, n.d.), p. 12.

[17] In the following account of this book that I give I have liberally raided two of the pages in an article of mine ("Maritain in His Role as Aesthetician") that appeared in *The Review of Metaphysics* in March, 1955 (Vol. VIII, No. 3). I am indebted to the Editor for permitting this act of plunder.

In this book, which grew out of his Mellon lectures that were given during 1952 in the National Gallery in Washington, Maritain brings to a point of culmination nearly forty years of study in the arts and in aesthetics. And in one of its aspects the book has it as a major concern to call into question the modern notion that the creative process in art is merely an *operational* process and that the artist is merely a special sort of technician. "As to the great artists," he says, "who take pleasure in describing themselves as mere engineers in the manufacturing of an artifact of words or sounds, as Paul Valéry did, and as Stravinsky does, I think that they purposely do not tell the truth, at least completely. In reality the spiritual content of a creative intuition, with the poetic or melodic sense it conveys, animates their artifact, despite their grudge against inspiration." [18] And this must be so, because, as Maritain insists, the activity which produces poetic art does not begin until the poet permits himself to be invaded by the reality of "Things" and until he himself seeks to invade the deepest recesses of his own subjectivity—the two movements of the spirit being performed together, as though one, "in a moment of affective union." When the soul thus comes into profound spiritual contact with itself and when it also enters into the silent and mysterious depths of Being, it is brought back to "the single root" of its powers, "where the entire subjectivity is, as it were, gathered in a state of expectation and virtual creativity." [19] And the whole experience becomes "a state of obscure . . . and sapid knowing." [20] Then,

> after the silent gathering a breath arises, coming not from
> the outside, but from the center of the soul—sometimes a

[18] *Creative Intuition in Art and Poetry* (New York, 1953), p. 62.
[19] *Ibid.*, p. 239.   [20] *Ibid.*

breath which is almost imperceptible, but compelling and powerful, through which everything is given in easiness and happy expansion; sometimes a gale bursting all of a sudden, through which everything is given in violence and rapture; sometimes the gift of the beginning of a song; sometimes an outburst of unstoppable words.[21]

And only when this point in the artistic process has been reached may *operation* begin. For the artist to initiate the processes of *operation* at any earlier point is for him "to put the instrumental and secondary before the principal and primary, and to search for an escape through the discovery of a new external approach and new technical revolutions, instead of passing first through the creative source . . ." [22] Then, what is produced is but "a corpse of a work of art—a product of academicism." [23] "If creative intuition is lacking," he says, "a work can be perfectly made, and it is nothing; the artist has nothing to say. If creative intuition is present, and passes, to some extent, into the work, the work exists and speaks to us, even if it is imperfectly made and proceeds from a man who has the habit of art and a hand which shakes." [24]

At "the single root" of the poetic process, then, there is a profound act of creative intuition. And in this cognitive act, says Maritain, the soul "suffers things more than it learns them," experiencing them "through resonance in subjectivity." The thing that is cognitively grasped is simply "some complex of concrete and individual reality, seized in the violence of its sudden self-assertion and in the total unicity" [25] that is constituted by "all the other realities which echo in this existent, and which it con-

[21] *Ibid.*, p. 243.   [22] *Ibid.*, p. 223.   [23] *Ibid.*, p. 63.   [24] *Ibid.*, p. 60.
[25] *Ibid.*, p. 126.

veys in the manner of a sign." [26] And it is the richness of this
imaginative prehension that gives life and power to the mathe-
matic of poetic form.

Maritain is, of course, a good Thomist, and therefore he does
not need to be reminded that art is "a virtue of the practical intellect" and that it requires "all the logic and shrewdness, self-
restraint and self-possession of working intelligence." [27] Indeed,
he insists upon the essential relationship between art and reason,
since it is reason that discovers the necessities in the nature of
the medium that must be observed in order for the work to be
brought into existence. But he also insists that the reason and the
calculation that are in the poet "are there only to handle fire," [28]
and that to grant them anything more than this purely instrumental function, simply for the sake of adherence to a puri-
tantical formalism and a spurious austerity, is to be guilty of a
gratuitous dogmatism.

Now many of us will doubtless find it difficult to accept Maritain's argument in this book in its entirety, for there are phases
of his psychology—particularly those that bear upon his doctrine
of the spiritual preconscious—that will surely strike us as ex-
ceedingly cumbersome and perhaps even obscurantist. And I have
adduced his testimony here not because it perfectly answers all of
the questions that he raises. But, at a time when it is too much
our habit to regard the medium as the single factor controlling the
poetic process, Maritain's formulation of the problem has the very
great merit of eloquently reminding us again of the actual primacy
in the process of *poetic vision*. He discloses to us, that is, a stratagem for declaring once again that it is not language which brings

[26] *Ibid.*   [27] *Ibid.*, p. 246.   [28] *Ibid.*, p. 218.

"meaning to birth" and which enables the mind "to order itself"
—not language, but *vision*.

Eliseo Vivas also helps us to some extent, I believe, with our
difficulties, when he reminds us that what is in part distinctive
about the artist is his "passion for order." [29] "Really, universally,"
said Henry James, "relations stop nowhere, and the exquisite
problem of the artist is eternally but to draw, by a geometry
of his own, the circle within which they shall happily *appear* to
do so." [30] That is to say, the artist wants to give a shape and a
significance to what Vivas calls "the primary data of experience." He wants to contain the rich plenitude of experience within
a pattern that will illumine and give meaning to its multifarious
detail and its bewildering contingency. But, of course, he cannot
discover such a pattern unless he has a vantage point from which
to view experience and by means of which his insights may be
given order and proportion. Which is to say that he can trans-
mute the viscous stuff of existential reality into the order of significant form only in accordance with what are his most fundamental beliefs about what is radically significant in life, and
these beliefs he will have arrived at as a result of all the dealings
that he has had with the religious and philosophical and moral
and social issues that the adventure of living has brought his
way. The imaginative writer's beliefs, to be sure, are very rarely
highly "propositional" in character: they do not generally involve a highly schematized set of ideas or a fully integrated
philosophic system. He customarily has something much less
abstract—namely, a number of sharp and deeply felt insights

[29] *Creation and Discovery*, p. 117.
[30] *The Art of the Novel: Critical Prefaces* (New York, 1934), p. 5.

into the meaning of the human story that control all his transactions with the world that lies before him. And it is by means of these insights that he discovers "the figure in the carpet."

Graham Greene, in his criticism, has often liked to observe that "Every creative writer worth our consideration, every writer who can be called in the wide eighteenth-century use of the term a poet, is a victim: a man given to an obsession," [31] or to what he sometimes calls a "ruling passion." And I take it that when he speaks in this way he has in mind the poet's habit of loyalty to some way of seeing things, by means of which he grapples and comes to terms with the tumultuous and fragmentary world that presses in upon him. That is to say, I assume that Greene has in mind the act of consent which the poet gives to some fundamental hypothesis about the nature of existence which itself in turn introduces structure and coherence for him into the formless stuff of life itself. And it is, indeed, I believe, this act that constitutes the real beginning of the poetic process: the rest is simply a matter of the kind of knowledgeable experimentation within the limits of his medium that the expert craftsman engages in till he discovers what he wants to say gaining incarnation within a given form.

Now I am aware that I must appear to be advocating a view of the poetic process which, in point of fact, I do not hold at all. That is to say, in much that I have just now said it may have seemed that I was implying that, before even initiating the purely literary task, it is necessary for the poet to do an enormous amount of thinking. I have attributed to the writer's metaphysic or his

[31] *The Lost Childhood* (New York, 1952), p. 79.

beliefs a decisive role in the creative process, and thus it would seem that I am saying that it is necessary for the writer to engage in a great deal of abstract thinking before that process can even be initiated. But this I do not think is true at all. I do not, of course, want to associate myself with that tendency in modern literary theory which supports the supposition that the writer is not a thinker at all. This is a notion which T. S. Eliot has, I suppose, done more than anyone else to foster, and it is simply another instance of the confusion which his criticism, great as it is, occasionally contains. In his famous essay on "Shakespeare and the Stoicism of Seneca" he tells us, for example, that the poet does not "think" but that he makes poetry out of thought and that, therefore, he cannot *as poet* be said to "believe" in the system of thought that lies behind his poetry. In the particular case with which he is dealing, he tells us that Shakespeare did not really "think," that he simply took the muddled and incompatible ideas of Seneca and Machiavelli and Montaigne and made poetry out of them. And Eliot having—and properly so—the enormous prestige in our time that he has, it is not surprising that our generation should have become for a time so convinced that Shakespeare was not a profound thinker, if he was a thinker at all, that he merely assimilated and felicitously reexpressed well-worn truisms. Or, again, in the case of Dante, he tells us that Dante did not "think" either, that he simply took the magnificent formulations of St. Thomas and used them as the foundation of his poem. But surely there is a great confusion here, for, as Martin Jarrett-Kerr has remarked, "If . . . we start from the initial conviction that one of the first marks of the major poet or

novelist is the possession of a *fine mind,* we must refuse to concede that Shakespeare or Dante did not think but had their
thinking done for them." [32]

Eliot's error here results, I suspect, from the supposition that
to acknowledge the poet as a thinker is in effect to say that the
poetic process originates in a highly developed *system* of ideas,
and this is, of course, not at all the case. What I have been calling
the writer's "beliefs" are rarely if ever the highly "propositional"
things that Eliot, in denying them the importance which I have
given them, seems to think they are. For what the writer generally has is not a *system* of belief but rather *an imagination* of
what is radically significant.

So, in insisting upon the writer's necessary dependence upon
his beliefs, I am not at all intending to suggest that the poet or
the novelist must, first of all, be a philosopher—though, on the
other hand, I am not at all in accord with Eliot's contention that
the poet is not really a thinker at all, a contention which is, by
the way, significantly contradicted by Eliot's own career in poetry.
There is a distinction somewhere in St. Thomas which illum-
inates, I think, the nature of the poet's relation to his beliefs. St.
Thomas distinguishes between *cognitio per modum cognitionis*
—knowledge, that is, in the manner of or by means of the intelligence or the discursive reason—and *cognitio per modum inclinationis,* knowledge, that is, in the manner of or by means of
inclination. And what I would suggest is that the poet holds his
"first principles" or his beliefs or his metaphysic *per modum inclinationis*—that is, inclinatorily. Which is to say that his beliefs
point in the direction of a coherent philosophy of life towards

[32] *Studies in Literature and Belief* (New York, 1955), p. 5.

which his sensibility has an irresistible inclination and in which it finds its necessary sanction. The contrast between the two modes of cognition is, to be sure, not an absolute contrast, and what it is therefore proper to say is that it is the *tendency* of the poet to hold his beliefs *per modum inclinationis,* though there are some writers, Eliot among them, who also hold their beliefs *per modum cognitionis.* But in whatever manner they may be held in the individual case, what I am now insisting upon principally is the precedence and the primacy of the act by which the poet searches experience and finds therein an ultimate concern that gives him then a perspective upon the flux and the flow.

Now whatever it is that concerns the poet ultimately, that constitutes his "ruling passion" and the substance of his *vision,* is something to which the critic can be attentive only as it is discoverable in the work. By now surely we have all taken to hear the lesson of Wimsatt and Beardsley on "The Intentional Fallacy," and we understand the irrelevance of any essay in literary criticism that is based upon some process of armchair psychoanalysis which seeks to elevate the biographical category of the artist's conscious intention into a category of aesthetic discrimination. But the designation of "intentionalism" as fallacious becomes itself a fallacy if it is made to support the view that a work of literary art is "a merely formal structure devoid of embodied meanings and values."[33] For such aesthetic objects, though "they may be found in the realm of pure design or pure music,"[34] simply do not exist in the realm of literature where surely a main part of the critic's task involves the discovery of "the actual operative intention which, as telic cause, accounts for the fin-

[33] Vivas, *Creation and Discovery,* p. 172.   [34] *Ibid.*

ished work"[35] and which can be defined only in terms of the vision of the world which it serves. The work of art, says De Rougemont, is a trap for the attention; but he also says that it is an "oriented trap." That is to say, the authentic work of literary art is a "trap," in the sense that, having the kind of autonomy that modern criticism has claimed for it, it "has for its specific function . . . the magnetizing of the sensibility, the fascinating of the meditation";[36] as Vivas would put it, it can command upon itself an act of "intransitive attention." But the trap is "oriented": it *focuses* the attention, that is, upon something which transcends the verbal structure itself, in those of its aspects that have claimed the poet's concern. And thus it is that the autonomy of the work is no more an absolute thing than is the intransitivity of the reader's attention, for both are qualified by the implicative relations that branch out indefinitely from the aesthetic fact towards the world by which that fact is surrounded.

Here it is, then, that we may discover the point of entry into the literary work that we have. For it is analysis of the sort that we have been conducting that reveals that the work is not a closed system and that it does not have that quality of "aseity" which Scholastic theologians have considered the Godhead to possess, by reason of the self-derived and eternally independent character of its being. The work is not wholly self-contained and utterly cut off from the reader, because, in the creative process, the aesthetic intentions of the artist are not segregated from all that most vitally concerns him as a human being but are, on the contrary, formed by these concerns and are thus empowered to orient the work

[35] *Ibid.*, p. 164.
[36] De Rougemont, "Religion and the Mission of the Artist," p. 176.

toward the common human experience. Imaginative literature does not speak about this experience, of course, in the way that science speaks of it: it does not give us propositions about it: the poet does not generally force upon us interpretations of it: "Poetry is not interpretation," as Archibald MacLeish has remarked in a recent essay.[37] The poet is distinguished not by his skill in expounding a thesis but rather by his skill in *rendering* the human story, in *dramatizing* it, in making it *concrete* before the gaze of the mind. He makes us *look* at the living body of the world, and the meaning of what we look at appears to be quite indistinct from the form in which it is presented to us—so much so, indeed, that, in describing the mode of poetry's existence, we feel compelled to use such language as modern criticism has made familiar and to speak of its "autonomy."

But to stress the fact that poetic art signifies *by means of its structure* need not, I think, commit us to a formalism so purist as to require the view that the autonomy of the work is absolute. For, as I have been insisting, great literature does, in point of fact, always open outward to the world, and that which keeps the universe of poetry from being hermetically sealed off from the universe of man is the poet's vision that it incarnates, of spaces and horizons, of cities and men, of time and eternity. This is why those modern theorists who tell us that the literary work is merely a verbal structure and that its analysis therefore involves merely a study of grammar and syntax—this is why they so completely miss the mark. They forget that writers use language with reference to what they know and feel and believe and that we can there-

[37] "The Language of Poetry," in *The Unity of Knowledge*, ed. by Lewis Leary (Garden City, N.Y., 1955), p. 230.

fore understand their poems and novels only if we have some
appreciation of how their beliefs have operated in enriching the
meaning of the words that they employ. The "poem-in-itself,"
in other words, as merely a structure of language, is simply a
naked abstraction, for the real poem, the real novel, is something that we begin to appropriate only as we seek some knowledge of the context of belief and the quality of vision out of
which it springs and with reference to which the words on the
printed page have their fullest and richest meaning.

Now we have, I think, arrived at the point in our argument at
which it is finally possible for me to turn immediately to the gen-
erality of my subject. For what I can now say is that the aspect of
poetic art to which I have been referring by the terms *vision* and
belief is precisely the element which we ought to regard as con-
stituting the religious dimension of imaginative literature. When
I speak of the religious dimension of literary art, in other words,
I do not have in mind any special iconical materials stemming
from a tradition of orthodoxy which may or may not appear in
a given work. For were it to be so conceived, it might indeed then
be something peripheral and inorganic to the nature of literature
itself; whereas the way of regarding our problem that I now want
to recommend is one that involves the proposal that the religious
dimension is something intrinsic to and constitutive of the nature
of literature as such. And I am here guided in my understanding
of what is religious in the orders of cultural expression by the
conception of the matter that has been so ably advanced by the
distinguished Protestant theologian Paul Tillich. In all the work
that he has done in the philosophy of culture over the past thirty

years the persistent strain that is to be noted is one that arises
out of his insistence upon what might be called the co-inherence
of religion and culture. He likes to say that "Religion is the substance of culture and culture the form of religion." [38] He has remarked, for example:

> If any one, being impressed by the mosaics of Ravenna or the
> ceiling paintings of the Sistine Chapel, or by the portraits of
> the older Rembrandt, should be asked whether his experience
> was religious or cultural, he would find the answer difficult.
> Perhaps it would be correct to say that his experience was
> cultural as to form, and religious as to substance. It is cultural
> because it is not attached to a specific ritual-activity; and re-
> ligious because it evokes questioning as to the Absolute or
> the limits of human existence. This is equally true of paint-
> ing, of music and poetry, of philosophy and science. . . .
> Wherever human existence in thought or action becomes a
> subject of doubts and questions, wherever unconditioned
> meaning becomes visible in works which only have condi-
> tioned meaning in themselves, there culture is religious.[39]

And Tillich has acknowledged that it is to the theoretical com-
prehension of this "mutual immanence of religion and culture"
that his philosophy of religion is primarily dedicated. "No cultural creation," he says, "can hide its religious ground," [40] and
its religious ground is formed by the "ultimate concern" to which
it bears witness, for that, he insists, is what religion is: it "is ultimate concern." [41] And since it is religion, in this sense, that is

---

[38] *The Protestant Era* (Chicago, 1948), p. 57.
[39] Tillich, *The Interpretation of History* (New York, 1936), p. 49.
[40] *The Protestant Era*, p. 57.   [41] *Ibid.*, p. 59.

truly substantive in the various symbolic expressions of a culture, the task of criticism, in whatever medium it may be conducted, is, at bottom, that of deciphering the given work at hand in such a way as to reveal the ultimate concern which it implies. For, as he says, in the depth of every cultural creation "there is an ultimate . . . and [an] all-determining concern, something absolutely serious," [42] even if it is expressed in what are conventionally regarded as secular terms.

It should, of course, be said that, in these definitions, Tillich is not seeking to *identify* religion and culture; but he does want to avoid the error that Eliot has cautioned us against, "of regarding religion and culture as two separate things between which there is a *relation*." [43] For what he recognizes is that the whole cultural process by which man expresses and realizes his rational humanity is actually governed by what are his most ultimate concerns—his concerns, that is, "with the meaning of life and with all the forces that threaten or support that meaning. . . ." [44] And, in passing, it is, I think, worth remarking that it is this profoundly realistic approach to the problem of cultural interpretation that enables Professor Tillich to see that in our own period the most radically religious movements in literature and painting and music may gain expression in strangely uncanonical terms— in despairing maledictions and in apocalyptic visions of "the abyss" of disintegration that threatens the world today. For, as he would say, in the very profundity with which *Wozzeck* and the *Guernica* and *The Waste Land* express the disorder of the times

[42] *Ibid.*, pp. 58–59.
[43] Eliot, *Notes Towards the Definition of Culture* (New York, 1949), pp. 31–32.
[44] James Luther Adams, "Tillich's Concept of the Protestant Era," Editor's Appendix in *The Protestant Era*, p. 273.

there is an equally profound witness to the spiritual order that has been lost, so that these great expressions of the modern movement in art are rather like a confused and uncertain prayer that corresponds to the second petition of the *Our Father*.[45]

We are now, then, brought to the point at which we must regather our bearings by a final act of recapitulation. We have said that the work of literary art is a special sort of linguistic structure that traps the attention intransitively; but we have also argued that the intransitivity of the reader's attention is not absolute, since the autonomy of the object which captures his attention is not itself absolute. The literary work is a trap, but it is a trap that is *oriented* toward the world of existence that transcends the work —and the work is *oriented* by the *vision*, by the *belief*, by the *ultimate concern* of which it is an incarnation: its *orientation*, that is to say, is essentially religious. And this is why criticism itself must, in the end, be theological. The prevailing orthodoxy in contemporary criticism, to be sure, generally represents hostility toward the idea of metaphysical and theological considerations being introduced into the order of critical discourse. But, as Leslie Fiedler has remarked:

> The "pure" literary critic, who pretends, in the cant phrase,
> to stay "inside" a work all of whose metaphors and meanings
> are pressing outward, is only half-aware. And half-aware, he
> deceives; for he cannot help smuggling unexamined moral
> and metaphysical judgments into his "close analyses," any

[45] De Rougemont says that "art would appear to be like an invocation (more often than not unconscious) to the lost harmony, like a prayer (more often than not confused), corresponding to the second petition of the Lord's prayer —'Thy Kingdom come.' " "Religion and the Mission of the Artist," p. 186.

more than the "pure" literary historian can help bootlegging
unconfessed aesthetic estimates into his chronicles. Literary
criticism is always becoming "something else," for the simple
reason that literature is always "something else." [46]

Our abdication from the reigning poetics of our time is, however, only partial, for the religious dimension of literature, as we
have defined it, must be regarded as something which, in so far
as it is really a datum for critical inspection and assessment, exists
in the language of the work. For the only thing that lies before
the critic is a composition in language, and, after all, it is, presumably, his skill in the supervision of language that *primarily*
distinguishes the literary artist: surely it would be wrongheaded
to assume that the thing that makes him an artist is the profundity or the novelty of his vision: no, he makes good his voca-
tional claim in the republic of letters by the extent of the success
with which he shapes the substance of experience, in accordance
with his vision of what it is that makes it ultimately meaningful. And he can give a significant form or shape to experience
only in so far as he takes the highest kind of advantage of the
medium in which his art is wrought. So it may, then, I think,
be taken for granted that whatever it is that *orients* a work of
literary art or that constitutes the *ultimate concern* that it embodies is something that will disclose itself in the ways in which
the writer brings the resources of language into the service of his
project. And thus we shall want very carefully to preserve all that
has been gained in modern criticism as a result of its methodo-

[46] "Toward an Amateur Criticism," *The Kenyon Review,* Vol. XII, No. 4
(Autumn, 1950), p. 564.

logical researches into the problem of how the language of imaginative literature is to be understood and talked about. But for the critic to insist upon remaining merely a kind of grammarian is for him to forgo many of the most interesting and significant discriminations that literary criticism can make. For, though the literary work is a special sort of linguistic structure, that which holds the highest interest for us is the special seizure of reality toward which this structure is instrumental. It is, in other words, the nature of literature itself that compels the critic finally to move beyond the level of verbal analysis to the level of metaphysical and theological valuation. On this level, of course, he can establish the propriety of his judgments only by reference to his own insight, his own scale of values, his own sense of what is important in art and in life. And, as the English critic S. L. Bethell once remarked,

> if he is a Christian worthy of the name, his whole outlook will be coloured by his religion; he will see life in Christian terms, and, though he may ignore an atheist writer's professed atheism, he will still judge his degree of insight into character by his own insight, which will have been formed in part by his Christian experience. And the non-Christian critic—let us be clear about this—will also judge a writer's insight into character (or into anything else, of course) by the standard of his own insight, however derived. There is no "impartial criticism" in this sense, or rather there is no critical neutrality; there are only Christian critics and Marxist critics and Moslem critics—and critics who think themselves disinterested but who are really swayed unconsciously by the

beliefs they have necessarily acquired by being members of a particular society in a particular place and time.[47]

And, as Bethell observed with great shrewdness,

the last are really the least impartial, for, believing themselves impartial, they are open to every unconscious influence upon their judgment, while the "doctrinaire" critic may keep his doctrine well in view and, if not entirely avoiding prejudice, may at least give his readers fair warning of what to expect.[48]

But now my reader at this point may well want to raise the question as to whether my use of these quotations from Bethell is calculated to suggest that we are justified in trying to guarantee literary art by the quality of belief that it possesses. And, were the question to be put to me, my impulse, as a Christian, would, I think, be to say, with Roy Battenhouse, that "the good poet should be able, like Adam in the Garden, to name every creature correctly. Apprehending the form of each thing that is brought before him, he should be able to assign it its proper place." [49] But, of course, this capacity, which so influentially determines the outcome of the artistic process, is itself very largely dependent upon the artist's metaphysical or religious orientation—so that, as a Christian, I should again feel prompted to say, with Battenhouse, that

[47] *Essays on Literary Criticism and the English Tradition* (London, 1948), p. 24–25.

[48] *Ibid.*, p. 25.

[49] "The Relation of Theology to Literary Criticism," *The Journal of Bible and Religion*, Vol. XIII, No. 1 (February, 1945), p. 20.

if it is true that the light with which an artist sees inclines to affect the justness of his observations, the presence of full light cannot but clarify the issues of proportion and order. With inadequate lighting, the artist will not see certain things he ought to see; it will be all too easy for him to draw disproportionately what he does see. To put it another way the artist who takes up his location in Plato's cave has not the same chance as he who sets up shop by Christ's open tomb.[50]

In principle, I should, in other words, expect the Christian reader at least—*all other things being equal*—more enthusiastically to give his suffrage to a literature that was Christianly *oriented* than to one which was not. But, now, not as a matter of principle but as a matter of fact, the Christian reader lives in a period whose characteristic quality, at least ever since the Renaissance, has been defined, as Erich Heller has reminded us, not merely by a dissociation of faith from knowledge but by what has been the profounder severance of faith from sensibility. "It is this rift," says Heller, "which has made it impossible for most Christians not to *feel,* or at least not to feel *also* as true many 'truths' which are incompatible with the truth of their faith." [51] They have, in other words, been in very much the same position that the father of the possessed child was in whom the Synoptist records as having cried out: "Lord, I believe: help thou mine unbelief" (Mark 9.24). And, this being the case, the Christian reader will *actually* respond to the various beliefs which literature may present with

[50] *Ibid.*
[51] *The Disinherited Mind: Essays in Modern German Literature and Thought* (Philadelphia, 1952), p. 125.

much the same latitudinarianism that any other sensitive reader in our time will bring to bear upon his dealings with literary art: that is to say, what he will principally require is that the view of life that is conveyed by the given poem or novel commend itself as a *possible* view, as one to which an intelligent and sensitive observer of the human scene *might* be led by a sober consideration of the facts of experience. And, though he will agree with Eliot that to judge a work of art by artistic standards and to judge it by religious standards ought to "come in the end to the same thing," [52] he will recognize, as Eliot does, that, in our time, this is an end at which none of us is likely to arrive.

[52] Eliot, *Notes Towards the Definition of Culture*, p. 29.

LOUIS L. MARTZ

Wallace Stevens: The World as Meditation

"In an age of disbelief," says Wallace Stevens in a late essay, "it is for the poet to supply the satisfactions of belief, in his measure and in his style." It is my purpose here to explore the nature of those satisfactions, to examine the measure and the style that Stevens achieved in his later poetry, and in this way to suggest the answer that Stevens found to his own blunt question: "What, then, is the nature of poetry in a time of disbelief?" [1]

The answer is implicit in the late poem that provides my theme and title here: *The World as Meditation* (1952) seems to sum up the poetical discoveries of Stevens since that time, some thirty years earlier, when his Paltry Nude started on her Spring Voyage through the world of *Harmonium,* to become at the close of that volume a complete Nomad Exquisite, fully attuned to the harmonies of nature, creating as nature herself creates:

As the immense dew of Florida
Brings forth

[1] "Two or Three Ideas" (1951), in *Opus Posthumous,* ed. by Samuel French Morse (New York, 1957), pp. 206, 211 (cited hereafter as OP).

The big-finned palm
And green vine angering for life,

. . . .

So, in me, come flinging
Forms, flames, and the flakes of flames.

The World as Meditation, on the other hand, finds its central
proposition, not in any text from the surface of things, but in
certain words of a human composer, Georges Enesco: "J'ai passé
trop de temps à travailler mon violon, à voyager. Mais l'exercice
essentiel du compositeur—la méditation—rien ne l'a jamais sus-
pendu en moi. . . . Je vis un rêve permanent, qui ne s'arrête ni
nuit ni jour." With those words as epigraph, the poem presents
as its symbol of human achievement the figure of Penelope, await-
ing the return of Ulysses. As the sun rises she awakens to the
meditation that has composed her life:

A form of fire approaches the cretonnes of Penelope,
Whose mere savage presence awakens the world in which she
    dwells.

She has composed, so long, a self with which to welcome him,
Companion to his self for her, which she imagined,
Two in a deep-founded sheltering, friend and dear friend.

. . . .

But was it Ulysses? Or was it only the warmth of the sun
On her pillow? The thought kept beating in her like her heart.
The two kept beating together. It was only day.

It was Ulysses and it was not. Yet they had met,
Friend and dear friend and a planet's encouragement.
The barbarous strength within her would never fail.

There is, we see, a "savage presence" outside her, the primitive force of the sun, which arouses within her a "barbarous strength," some primitive human power that makes it possible for her to compose a self, with the sun's encouragement; and so she dwells in a world of belief created by her will. This sounds like the conception found at the close of Stevens's essay "The Noble Rider" (1942), where he mentions a certain nobility of mind that constitutes "a violence from within that protects us from a violence without. It is the imagination pressing back against the pressure of reality." Thus the violence of the sun might have aroused Penelope to the violent, ugly pressure of those outward suitors; but her imagination of Ulysses, her constant meditation of reunion with the man she constantly creates in her mind, this power presses back, composes within herself a world of value and order. Thus, as Stevens concludes in that essay, imagination "seems, in the last analysis, to have something to do with our self-preservation." [2]

I have used two terms, both prominent in Stevens's writings: *imagination, meditation;* they are not synonymous. Meditation is the essential exercise which, constantly practiced, brings the imagination into play, releases creative power, enables the human being to compose a sensitive, intelligent and generous self. It is the sort of self that Stevens has found fully represented in the person of George Santayana, as he points out in an essay of 1948. "Most men's lives," he regretfully concedes, "are thrust upon them" by the outward violence; but he insists:

> There can be lives, nevertheless, which exist by the deliberate choice of those that live them. To use a single illustration: it may be assumed that the life of Professor Santayana is a

[2] *The Necessary Angel* (New York, 1951), p. 36 (cited hereafter as NA).

life in which the function of the imagination has had a function similar to its function in any deliberate work of art or
letters. We have only to think of this present phase of it, in
which, in his old age, he dwells in the head of the world, in
the company of devoted women, in their convent, and in the
company of familiar saints, whose presence does so much to
make any convent an appropriate refuge for a generous and
human philosopher. [NA, 147–48]

And so in his late poem *To an Old Philosopher in Rome* (1952)
he finds the fulfillment of human existence in Santayana's rec-
onciliation of flesh and spirit on the threshold of death:

> The sounds drift in. The buildings are remembered.
> The life of the city never lets go, nor do you
> Ever want it to. It is part of the life in your room.
> Its domes are the architecture of your bed.
>
> .   .   .   .
>
> It is a kind of total grandeur at the end,
> With every visible thing enlarged and yet
> No more than a bed, a chair and moving nuns,
> The immensest theatre, the pillared porch,
> The book and candle in your ambered room,
>
> Total grandeur of a total edifice,
> Chosen by an inquisitor of structures
> For himself. He stops upon this threshold,
> As if the design of all his words takes form
> And frame from thinking and is realized.

Such admiration for the power of *thinking,* for the constructive
power of deliberate choice—this is not the sort of values that

were being attributed to Stevens fifteen or twenty years ago. The central impact of Stevens's poetry up to about 1940 has been, I think, admirably summed up by Yvor Winters in his famous essay "Wallace Stevens or The Hedonist's Progress." There Winters, basing his thesis primarily on *Harmonium,* saw in Stevens the cultivation of "the realm of emotion divorced from understanding," the commendation of "the emotions as a good in themselves." It was, he felt, a point of view that had led Stevens from the great poetry of *Harmonium* into a "rapid and tragic decay" of style, the sad, inevitable progress of the hedonist, "unable to think himself out of the situation into which he has wandered." [3]

Winters has made a brilliant diagnosis of the malady; but he underestimated the patient's will to live. Looking back now, with the immense advantage of all that Stevens has published since Winters wrote, and with the equally great advantage of the recent *Opus Posthumous*—looking back now, we can see that something quite different happened. We can see something analogous to the course of Yeats's poetry. We can see a poet, by a deliberate process of self-knowledge, rebuilding himself and his poetry, rebuilding himself through his poetry, and achieving, in *Transport to Summer* (1947), a volume of meditative poetry that is in every way the equal of his great, first volume of hedonist poetry. It is not a question of setting up divisions, but of watching recessive elements in the early poetry develop into dominance.

Let us try to sketch, now, this different progress. Stevens's second volume, *Ideas of Order,* appeared in 1935; its slimness, its dominant tone, and its title are all significant of a change in the poet's outlook. The buoyancy that gave forth the bounty of *Harmonium* is gone; that force within, like "the immense dew

---

[3] *The Anatomy of Nonsense* (Norfolk, Conn., 1943), pp. 89, 91, 97.

of Florida," that had brought forth "Forms, flames, and the flakes of flames" is subsiding, although here and there it reappears, the old gay defiance of Winters:

> But what are radiant reason and radiant will
> To warblings early in the hilarious trees
> Of summer, the drunken mother?

Or:

> What is there here but weather, what spirit
> Have I except it comes from the sun?

The trouble is that the younger Nomad Exquisite had lived by a view that the poet of the 1930s could no longer accept, for reasons he suggests in the late essay cited at the outset of this discussion: "If in the minds of men creativeness was the same thing as creation in the natural world, if a spiritual planet matched the sun, or if without any question of a spiritual planet, the light and warmth of spring revitalized all our faculties, as in a measure they do, all the bearings one takes, all the propositions one formulates would be within the scope of that particular domination"—as they were, for the most part, in *Harmonium*. "The trouble is, however, that men in general do not create in light and warmth alone," he continues. "They create in darkness and coldness. They create when they are hopeless, in the midst of antagonisms, when they are wrong, when their powers are no longer subject to their control. They create as the ministers of evil" (OP, 210). *Ideas of Order* moves in this different world; it is filled with the tones of evening: *A Fading of the Sun, Gray Stones and Gray Pigeons, Autumn Refrain, Winter Bells, Sad Strains of a Gay Waltz.*

> There is order in neither sea nor sun.
> The shapes have lost their glistening.
> There are these sudden mobs of men.

In this new atmosphere one poem stands out to control the chaos: the famous *Idea of Order at Key West*. Here the speaker, significantly, stands at the far edge of Florida, his back upon that world of flame and green. The physical world now offers none of its old "comforts of the sun," but exists here as

> The meaningless plungings of water and the wind,
> Theatrical distances, bronze shadows heaped
> On high horizons, mountainous atmospheres
> Of sky and sea.

The object of wonder and admiration is now a human figure, that singer by the shore whose voice made

> The sky acutest at its vanishing.
> She measured to the hour its solitude.
> She was the single artificer of the world
> In which she sang.

This is more than the Palace of Hoon, the solipsist of *Harmonium;* for the idea of order here resides in more than mental landscapes, in "More even than her voice, and ours": the idea of order is found in a unique conjunction of landscape, singer, and listener, a situation in which the listener's mind, exulting in the full strength of its powers, is able to assert the controlling force of consciousness, "Fixing emblazoned zones and fiery poles" upon the outer atmosphere, "Arranging, deepening, enchanting night"—while realizing fully that the outer universe goes its inhuman way.

The fierce strength of mind in that poem, its clipped and muted language before the final exultation, prepares the way for a striking addition to the volume *Ideas of Order,* when it appeared in a trade edition in the next year, 1936. The volume no longer opens with the curiously fatigued poem, *Sailing after Lunch,* where Stevens truly says, "My old boat goes round on a crutch / And doesn't get under way," and where he ends with the sentimental desire:

> To expunge all people and be a pupil
> Of the gorgeous wheel and so to give
> That slight transcendence to the dirty sail.

No, the volume now opens with the stirring *Farewell to Florida,* in which Stevens renounces all that "Florida" has symbolized in his earlier poetry: that world of vivid physical apprehension, where man created within the bounds of the natural order. "Her mind had bound me round," he says, but now he cries:

> Go on, high ship, since now, upon the shore,
> The snake has left its skin upon the floor.
> Key West sank downward under massive clouds
> And silvers and greens spread over the sea. The moon
> Is at the mast-head and the past is dead.
> Her mind will never speak to me again.

And he looks forward to his engagement with a new, a tough, bitter, and turbulent subject:

> My North is leafless and lies in a wintry slime
> Both of men and clouds, a slime of men in crowds.
> The men are moving as the water moves,
> This darkened water cloven by sullen swells

Against your sides, then shoving and slithering,
The darkness shattered, turbulent with foam.
To be free again, to return to the violent mind
That is their mind, these men, and that will bind
Me round, carry me, misty deck, carry me
To the cold, go on, high ship, go on, plunge on.

Stevens, it is clear, has determined to take his old boat out of
The Pleasures of Merely Circulating, to plunge into the turmoil
of the mid-thirties, to engage it somehow in his poetry. In fact,
he had already begun the effort. The year before *Farewell to
Florida* appeared he had already published the first part of what
was to become his longest poetical effort, *Owl's Clover,* which appeared in 1936 in its original version of 861 lines. It is a poem
that caused Stevens immense labor and, finally, intense dissatisfaction. In 1937 it reappeared with nearly 200 lines cut out; and
in 1954 Stevens omitted it entirely from his *Collected Poems,* on
the grounds that it was "rhetorical," Mr. Morse tells us (OP, xxiii).
As a result of this drastic omission, the reader of the *Collected
Poems* may emerge with a sense of the poet's steady self-possession, an ideal progress from the old gaudy style toward a sober,
muted, thoughtful, pruned, and thoroughly remade poetry: for
we move from *Ideas of Order* directly into *The Man with the
Blue Guitar,* where

The man bent over his guitar,
A shearsman of sorts.

A shearsman indeed, a sort of tailor, cutting his cloth anew and
shearing away the excess.[4] But the effect is too neat. We need

---

[4] See Stevens's explanation of this figure in a letter to his Italian translator,
Renato Poggioli: "This refers to the posture of the speaker, squatting like a

Owl's Clover, preferably in its first version, to tell us all the trouble of the change; and fortunately we have it all now before us once again, in the new posthumous volume. It is not a successful poem, though it contains great passages and opens remarkably well, with the firmly controlled symbols of *The Old Woman and the Statue.* There the magnificent statue in the park represents the soaring, noble imagination of the past, "leaping in the storms of light": the statue is a work of art subtly and powerfully arranged for the human mind to grasp and be exalted. One thing, one thing only, the sculptor "had not foreseen": the old woman, "the bitter mind / In a flapping cloak," a woman so depressed that she cannot apprehend the statue's action:

> A woman walking in the autumn leaves,
> Thinking of heaven and earth and of herself
> And looking at the place in which she walked,
> As a place in which each thing was motionless
> Except the thing she felt but did not know.

That thing is the "harridan self," "Crying against a need that pressed like cold, / Deadly and deep." It is not simply physical poverty that tortures this suffering self: it is that she lives, as the second part tells us, amid "the immense detritus of a world"

> That is completely waste, that moves from waste
> To waste, out of the hopeless waste of the past
> Into a hopeful waste to come.

The hopeful waste of the future, I think, alludes to the sort of world proffered by Mr. Burnshaw, whose name adorns the origi-

---

tailor (a shearsman) as he works on his cloth." *Mattino Domenicale ed Altre Poesie* (Turin, 1954), p. 174.

nal title of the second part: *Mr. Burnshaw and the Statue* (later altered to *The Statue at the World's End*). Stanley Burnshaw was the Marxist critic who in 1935 had reviewed *Ideas of Order* with considerable acuteness, though with a condescending tone: he had seen it as a book of "speculations, questionings, contradictions"—"the record of a man who, having lost his footing, now scrambles to stand up and keep his balance." [5] The critique, being so largely true, left the mark, as *Owl's Clover* shows in its derisive rejection of all mass-solutions that offer only "an age of concentric mobs." But what can be offered instead to the suffering self? The offering in this long second section turns out, in spite of its high rhetoric, to be surprisingly meager: it is simply the old pleasures of Florida, chanted in a weak imitation of the old hieratic style of *Sunday Morning,* as this passage (later removed) indicates:

> Dance, now, and with sharp voices cry, but cry
> Like damsels daubed and let your feet be bare
> To touch the grass and, as you circle, turn
> Your backs upon the vivid statue. Then,
> Weaving ring in radiant ring and quickly, fling
> Yourselves away and at a distance join
> Your hands held high and cry again, but cry,
> This time, like damsels captured by the sky,
> Seized by that possible blue.

But those waltzes had ended, long since. Clearly, the poet must try another way, and so, in his third section, Stevens turns to develop a contrast between two ways of life. One is the old way of religious meditation, where "each man,"

[5] *New Masses,* Oct. 1, 1935, p. 42.

Through long cloud-cloister-porches, walked alone,
Noble within perfecting solitude,
Like a solitude of the sun, in which the mind
Acquired transparence and beheld itself
And beheld the source from which transparence came.

And the other is something that seems to have arisen or to be
arising in place of the old religious way, something he calls
Africa, a world of dense, savage, mindless animality, where

Death, only, sits upon the serpent throne:
Death, the herdsman of elephants,
To whom the jaguars cry and lions roar
Their petty dirges of fallen forest-men,
Forever hunting or hunted, rushing through
Endless pursuit or endlessly pursued,
Until each tree, each evil-blossomed vine,
Each fretful fern drops down a fear like dew.

From here on, in the middle of the poem, *Owl's Clover* provides
less and less sustenance for the troubled mind trying to feed in
the dark. It becomes increasingly turgid and incoherent. The old
religion cannot cope with "Africa," nor can the old art of the
statue; nor can the problems be met by the believers in necessity,
the nostalgic admirers of the old pioneer spirit, or the worshippers
of the "newest Soviet reclame." "How shall we face the edge of
time?"

Where shall we find more than derisive words?
When shall lush chorals spiral through our fire
And daunt that old assassin, heart's desire?

"Lush chorals"—the backward glance toward the days of *Harmonium*—is ominous, and we are not surprised to find the poem ending with a Sombre Figuration in which the poet attempts to find refuge in a vague, semi-Jungian concept of the "subman." This subman is some inner man of imagination, who lies below the torments of thought: "The man below the man below the man, / Steeped in night's opium, evading day." But the subman has a precarious tenure, for he seems to reside only in a rhetoric of empty assertion:

> And memory's lord is the lord of prophecy
> And steps forth, priestly in severity,
> Yet lord, a mask of flame, the sprawling form
> A wandering orb upon a path grown clear.

It is a relief to turn from this evasive subman to the daylight figure who shears away this outworn pomp. The sounds made by *The Man with the Blue Guitar* (1937) show that Stevens, within a year's hard thought, has taken quick, firm strides toward the position thoroughly established in his prose essays and his later poetry: that "the poet must get rid of the hieratic in everything that concerns him," that he must abolish "the false conception of the imagination as some incalculable *vates* within us, unhappy Rodomontade" (NA, 58, 61)—i.e. the opium-drugged subman must be erased, along with the style in which he had been expressed. In his place we will have something like Picasso's clear, clean image of the old Guitar Player, a product of his "blue period" (though the guitar itself happens to be tan), which was, incidentally, exhibited in Hartford in 1934. We will have an image of life explored, discovered and developed through a language made out

of "things exactly as they are," a language moving now with a
tough intent toward the discovery of a self:

> Ah, but to play man number one,
> To drive the dagger in his heart,
>
> To lay his brain upon the board
> And pick the acrid colors out,
>
> To nail his thought across the door,
> Its wings spread wide to rain and snow,
>
> To strike his living hi and ho,
> To tick it, tock it, turn it true,
>
> To bang it from a savage blue,
> Jangling the metal of the strings.

This is as far as we can get from the puzzled, ruminative ebb
and flow of *Owl's Clover,* with its dissolving, eddying, and often
turbid blank verse: note here the crisp common diction, the
strict driving rhythm of the short couplets, subtly bound together by irregular rhymes and half-rhymes, all focused on one
aim: a definition of the *self* as the only province of poetry:

> Ourselves in the tune as if in space,
> Yet nothing changed, except the place
>
> Of things as they are and only the place
> As you play them, on the blue guitar,

> Placed, so, beyond the compass of change,
> Perceived in a final atmosphere;
>
> For a moment final.

We have returned to the central position of the *Idea of Order at Key West:* man's inner rage for order as the ultimate constructive force in man's universe, and hence the never-ending effort of the mind to control, within the mind, that outer monster, the inhuman universe:

> That I may reduce the monster to
> Myself, and then may be myself
>
> In face of the monster, be more than part
> Of it, more than the monstrous player of
>
> One of its monstrous lutes, not be
> Alone, but reduce the monster and be,
>
> Two things, the two together as one.

From this effort, he says, "I shall evolve a man."

This sequence of thirty-three tightly argued, tightly ordered meditations on a theme establishes the altered style of the later Stevens. He has here, in a deliberate act of choice, sheared away the kind of writing that he later calls "The romantic intoning, the declaimed clairvoyance," since this, he says, is the "appropriate idiom" of apotheosis; and this is not at all his subject now. Apotheosis elevates the mortal to the stature of divinity; it glorifies; and the appropriate poetry of apotheosis is therefore the hymn, the ode, the celebration, the chant. In a peculiar sense, this had been the appropriate idiom of his earlier poetry, since he was there attempting to show, as he tells the lady in *Sunday Morning,* that "Divinity must live within" the human realm: "Passions of rain, or moods in falling snow." Hence he uses the idiom of romantic intoning to glorify the satisfactions of this earth, often with deliberate irony: the Comedian speaks of his "first central hymns, the celebrants / Of rankest trivia"; and indeed the whole mock-heroic effect of the Comedian arises from the application of such grand intoning to the achievements of this "merest minuscule."

But in his new effort to evolve a man, a new idiom must be invented, since "apotheosis is not / The origin of the major man" for whom the poet is now searching. "He comes," says Stevens, "from reason, / Lighted at midnight by the studious eye, / Swaddled in revery." He is the meditative man, master of the essential exercise, student, scholar, rabbi of a new idiom, which Stevens in *Of Modern Poetry* (1940) calls "The poem of the mind in the act of finding / What will suffice." There has never been a better definition of what might be called the genre of meditative poetry. It is not, we note, a poem celebrating what suffices; nor is it any lamentation for the lack of what suffices. The difference between the true meditative poem and other poetic genres seems to be exactly this: that it alone represents "The poem of the act of the mind," the poem of the mind, in the very act of finding. One thinks of Emily Dickinson, of Hopkins, of George Herbert, and especially of Donne, in his *Divine Meditations* (*Holy Sonnets*).

But further definition of the genre, if there is really such a genre, is necessary, and Stevens suggests it all in *Of Modern Poetry*:

> It has to be living, to learn the speech of the place.
> It has to face the men of the time and to meet
> The women of the time. It has to think about war
> And it has to find what will suffice. It has
> To construct a new stage. It has to be on that stage
> And, like an insatiable actor, slowly and
> With meditation, speak words that in the ear,
> In the delicatest ear of the mind, repeat,
> Exactly, that which it wants to hear, at the sound
> Of which, an invisible audience listens,
> Not to the play, but to itself, expressed
> In an emotion as of two people, as of two
> Emotions becoming one.

Let me expand, with only a little liberty, the possible implications of that text. This kind of poetry must know the common speech; it must make contact with men in their normal existence, through its language, its images, and its consideration of urgent problems, such as war, of whatever kind, whether between man and man, or between body and soul, good and evil, man and his environment—the "war between the mind and sky" that Stevens describes at the end of his "Notes toward a Supreme Fiction." It has to find what will suffice, but in order to do this, it must construct a stage on which an actor may enact the process of this finding. And as this actor speaks his meditated words, they find a growing response in a certain invisible audience, which is not simply us, the readers or listeners, but is first of all the larger, total mind of the poet himself, controlling the actor, who is some projected aspect of himself. Then, in the close, that actor and that audience, projected self and larger self, come together in a moment of emotional resolution—for a moment final. It is a process that Stevens describes thus in his *Adagia:* "When the mind is like a hall in which thought is like a voice speaking, the voice is always that of someone else." The voice is that of some projected self: the audience is the whole self. "It is necessary to propose an enigma to the mind," he says in another adage. "The mind always proposes a solution" (OP, 168). All this seems to describe something very like the action in *The Idea of Order at Key West:* the landscape is the stage, the singer by the shore is the actor, and the poet's larger mind is the audience. It is also very like the action that one finds in Donne's *Holy Sonnets,* which we may take as a prime example of pure meditative poetry, since they seem to arise directly from the rigorous meditative exercises commonly practiced by religious men of the seventeenth century. Recall how Donne projects some aspect of himself upon a stage: the deathbed, the round earth's imagined corners, the Cross; how he then allows that self to ponder the given situation; and how, at the close, the projected self makes a subtle union with the whole mind of the poet, concluding all in the finding of what will suffice.

One can only ponder the possibilities here, and pause to stress one point. In formal religious meditation, as developed during Donne's time and later practiced (certainly) by Hopkins and (presumably) by Eliot, the process of meditation consists of

THE WORLD AS MEDITATION

something akin to that just described by Stevens. It begins with the deliberate creation of a setting and the placing of an actor there: some aspect of the self; this is the famous composition of place recommended by the Jesuit exercises. This is followed by predominantly intellectual analysis of some crucial problem pertaining to that self; and it all ends in a highly emotional resolution where the projected self and the whole mind of the meditator come together in a spirit of devotion. This threefold process is related to the old division of the soul into memory, understanding, and will; the exercise of meditation integrates these faculties.

How is it that a modern poet such as Wallace Stevens, so vastly different from the seventeenth century in the objects of his belief, should come to describe the need for a kind of poetry to which Donne's *Holy Sonnets* seem to belong: a kind that we might call the genre of meditative poetry? Donne's strenuous cultivation of this kind of poetry seems to be part of his lifelong effort to transcend and resolve his grievous sense of the fickleness, the dissolution, the transiency and fragility of all physical things. In Stevens, I think, an analogous situation called forth the analogous discipline. Stevens, in mid-career, recognized the dissolution, or the inadequacy, of his old poetic self—a recognition recorded with a wry gaiety in *The Comedian as the Letter C.* His later poems represent a rigorous search for ways and means of evolving another kind of poetic self, in accord with the outlook expressed in the late essay dealing with the "time of disbelief": "There was always in every man the increasingly human self, which instead of remaining the observer, the non-participant, the delinquent, became constantly more and more all there was or so it seemed; and whether it was so or merely seemed so still left it for him to resolve life and the world in his own terms" (OP, 207).

Allusions in his prose essays indicate that in this effort Stevens engaged in broad reading among tough thinkers, while all his later poetry displays a new respect for the "radiant idea" and the "radiant will." This is clear in the first part of *Notes toward a Supreme Fiction* (1942), which insists that the fiction must be, in some sense, "abstract." Not, I think, abstract in the usual sense of a philosophical abstraction; Stevens has told us plainly what he thinks of this in his *Landscape with Boat,* where he decries the man who "wanted imperceptible air," who "wanted the eye to see"

> And not be touched by blue. He wanted to know,
> A naked man who regarded himself in the glass
> Of air, who looked for the world beneath the blue,
> Without blue, without any turquoise tint or phase,
> Any azure under-side or after-color.

By "abstract" Stevens seems rather to imply a quality of being taken out, abstracted in the root sense, from that world we call the outer universe: something concrete taken out of this and taken into the mind through a process of full, exact realization. From that "local abstraction" the turquoise tints and azure undersides can then radiate in all directions. This is the process that Stevens vividly describes in section VII of *Credences of Summer,* where he begins by scorning those who have found it too hard "to sing in face / Of the object," and have therefore fled to the woods, where they could sing "their unreal songs, / Secure."

In a violent reversal of mood, he advocates a fiercely opposite process:

> Three times the concentred self takes hold, three times
> The thrice concentred self, having possessed
>
> The object, grips it in savage scrutiny,
> Once to make captive, once to subjugate
> Or yield to subjugation, once to proclaim
> The meaning of the capture, this hard prize,
> Fully made, fully apparent, fully found.

If this bears some resemblance to the old threefold process of formal meditation, it is only because Stevens has discovered for himself the same faculties, and has taught himself a way of using them for his own meditative ends. He has, in an essay of 1943, come to define the imagination as "the sum of our faculties," and has gone on to speak of "The acute intelligence of the imagination, the illimitable resources of its memory, its power to possess the moment it perceives" (NA, 61).

Indeed, it appears that Stevens has been thoroughly aware of the analogy I am suggesting, for in a newly published essay, written about 1937, we find him declaring: "The poet who wishes to contemplate the good in the midst of confusion is like the mystic who wishes to contemplate God in the midst of evil. . . . Resistance to the pressure of ominous and destructive circumstance consists of its conversion, so far as possible, into a different, an explicable, an amenable circumstance." And in this search, he adds, the poets "purge themselves before reality . . . in what they intend to be saintly exercises" (OP, 225, 227).

But if we accept Stevens's use of the term *meditation* as a proper description of his own secular exercises, we may appear to be stretching the word beyond any useful signification. Cannot any poem that contains any degree of hard thinking be thus called meditative? I do not think so, if we keep in mind the careful distinctions made by the old spiritual writer, François de Sales. "Every meditation is a thought," he says, "but every thought is not a meditation; for we have thoughts, to which our mind is carried without aim or design at all, by way of a simple musing. . . . And be this kind of thought as attentive as it may be, it can never bear the name of meditation." On the other hand, he says, "Sometimes we consider a thing attentively to learn its causes, effects, qualities; and this thought is named study." But "when we think of heavenly things, not to learn, but to delight in them, that is called to meditate; and the exercise thereof meditation." "So that meditation," he concludes, "is an attentive thought repeated or voluntarily maintained in the mind, to arouse the will to holy and wholesome affections and resolutions." [6]

It seems valid to adapt this definition to the meditation of earthly things, since meditation is a process, not a subject. If we do this, then Stevensian meditation becomes: attentive thinking about concrete things with the aim of developing an affectionate understanding of how good it is to be alive. We can see the process working everywhere in his later poetry, but nowhere better than in *The World as Meditation*, which now needs to be read entire as an example of the full development of Stevens's meditative style. Note first how far the poem's range extends be-

[6] François de Sales, *A Treatise on the Love of God* (1616), Book vi, chap. ii; adapted from the translation of 1630.

yond the "comforts of the sun": the verbal beauty of Enesco's French draws in the cosmopolitan world of the musician, as the figure of Penelope draws in the ancient world of legend. Yet the sun exists as first cause; without it there would be nothing. Thus the poem is phrased to allow a double reference: the sun is Penelope's companion, along with Ulysses. Note too how the poem fulfills all of Stevens's requirements for this modern poetry: common speech, common images, common problems; the establishment of a stage, the placing of Penelope as actor on that stage, the imputed working of her meditative thoughts, along with the constant presence of the poet's larger mind, controlling all, and concluding all with an affectionate understanding of what will suffice.

> Is it Ulysses that approaches from the east,
> The interminable adventurer? The trees are mended.
> That winter is washed away. Someone is moving
>
> On the horizon and lifting himself up above it.
> A form of fire approaches the cretonnes of Penelope,
> Whose mere savage presence awakens the world in which
>   she dwells.
>
> She has composed, so long, a self with which to welcome him,
> Companion to his self for her, which she imagined,
> Two in a deep-founded sheltering, friend and dear friend.
>
> The trees had been mended, as an essential exercise
> In an inhuman meditation, larger than her own.
> No winds like dogs watched over her at night.

She wanted nothing he could not bring her by coming alone.
She wanted no fetchings. His arms would be her necklace
And her belt, the final fortune of their desire.

But was it Ulysses? Or was it only the warmth of the sun
On her pillow? The thought kept beating in her like her
    heart.
The two kept beating together. It was only day.

It was Ulysses and it was not. Yet they had met,
Friend and dear friend and a planet's encouragement.
The barbarous strength within her would never fail.

She would talk a little to herself as she combed her hair,
Repeating his name with its patient syllables,
Never forgetting him that kept coming constantly so near.

The world of *Harmonium* has not been discarded here, but its
reliance on the natural force of "sensibility" has been modified,
and the pleasures of that world have been included within a
larger structure of existence. By 1951 Stevens could strongly question "the dogma that the origins of poetry are to be found in
the sensibility," and could suggest: "if one says that a fortunate
poem or a fortunate painting is a synthesis of exceptional concen-
tration . . . we find that the operative force within us does not,
in fact, seem to be the sensibility, that is to say, the feelings. It
seems to be a constructive faculty, that derives its energy more
from the imagination than from the sensibility"—imagination
being, as we have seen, the "sum of our faculties." But he adds,
in his cautious way, "I have spoken of questioning, not of deny-

ing" (NA, 164). That is because the old dews of Florida have
never ceased to affect him. One of his very last poems, *Prologues
to What Is Possible,* suggests that the value of existence may have
resided in

> A flick which added to what was real and its vocabulary,
> The way some first thing coming into Northern trees
> Adds to them the whole vocabulary of the South,
> The way the earliest single light in the evening sky, in spring,
> Creates a fresh universe out of nothingness by adding itself,
> The way a look or a touch reveals its unexpected magnitudes.

There is no inconsistency here. The look, the touch, the flick
of feeling, the "times of inherent excellence," "incalculable balances," "not balances / That we achieve but balances that hap-
pen"—these are things worth recognizing, and Stevens never
ceases to celebrate them as part of the wonder of human consciousness. But he is quick to recognize that "the casual is not
/ Enough": it does not attain the full "freshness of ourselves";
it does not satisfy the "will to make iris frettings on the blank."
Beyond the casual apprehensions there lie the willed and reasoned
structures of the mind, which Stevens presents in two forms. One
structure occurs when the mind thoroughly and fully concen-
trates upon the realization of some composition that appears to
be inherent in the external scene, as in *Credences of Summer.*

> Let's see the very thing and nothing else.
> Let's see it with the hottest fire of sight.
> Burn everything not part of it to ash.
>
> Trace the gold sun about the whitened sky
> Without evasion by a single metaphor.

Thus:

> One of the limits of reality
> Presents itself in Oley when the hay,
> Baked through long days, is piled in mows. It is
> A land too ripe for enigmas, too serene.

This seems to be what Stevens means by seeing things in their "first idea," their "ever-early candor"; this is the adequacy of landscape—for a moment final. It exists beyond us, it is no metaphor, and yet, Stevens insists, "the first idea is an imagined thing," since it is achieved by a calculated effort of the mind. It is part, then, "of the never-ending meditation," a poem of the mind in the act of finding what will suffice. It may be, he says, "of a man skating, a woman dancing, a woman / Combing," a Woman Looking at a Vase of Flowers, a Dish of Peaches in Russia, or a Large Red Man Reading: it may be found "in the crackling summer night,"

> In the *Duft* of towns, beside a window, beside
> A lamp, in a day of the week, the time before spring,
> A manner of walking, yellow fruit, a house,
> A street.

They are acts available to any man, a sort of poetry, "an imaginative activity that diffuses itself throughout our lives" (NA, 149). You return, say, from a long vacation with your family in the mountains, dog-tired, addle-brained, and feeling the whole expedition was a huge mistake. Two weeks later, the snapshots return, developed in full color: you are amazed at the beauty, the order, the focus; the trip is a success, after all. Such a realization would be, in Stevens's terms, a poetic action.

And finally, beyond such compositions, there lies the inex-
haustible "realm of resemblance," in which the faculties of the
imagination, using all their powers, "extend the object" by analogy, by metaphor. It is a realm in which the whole mind, like
Stevens's Penelope, uses the world of sensory experience as a base
upon which to construct a total edifice involving and demanding
the whole stretch of human experience. By the use of such anal-
ogies man connects the external and the internal; the action of
analogy is the mind's ultimate way of establishing its dominant,
controlling position amid the "moving chaos that never ends."
And this, too, is an activity that Stevens sees as available to everyone.

You sit in a chair, say, admiring the beauty of your four-year-old
daughter: you call to mind certain resemblances between her and
her absent mother, between her and your imagined image of yourself, between her and your memories and pictures of grandpar-
ents. You think, too, of certain painted images of children by
Renoir or Romney; you think of Andrew Marvell's *Picture of
Little T. C. in a Prospect of Flowers;* you think of the dogwood
that bloomed last Spring and of the zinnias now blooming outside. And for a moment the object toward which all these resemblances converge, or from which they infinitely extend—for
a moment the object becomes a vital center through which the
sense of life is composed, final: "completed in a completed scene,"
as Stevens says. Such is Wallace Stevens's *World as Meditation,* a
world where the poet may adopt the words of Valéry's Architect
and say, "By dint of constructing, . . . I truly believe that I have
constructed myself."

A Selected Bibliography

Abercrombie, Lascelles. The Theory of Poetry. London, 1924.
Chap. vi.

Abrams, M. H. The Mirror and the Lamp. New York, 1953.
Chaps. x–xi.

Aikin, Henry David, "The Aesthetic Relevance of Belief," *The Journal of Aesthetics and Art Criticism,* Vol. IX (1950–1951).

Adler, Alfred, "In What Sense Can Poetic Meaning Be Verified?" *Essays in Criticism,* Vol. II (1952).

Baker, Howard, "Belief and Dogma," *Hound and Horn,* Vol. XII (1933).

Belgion, Montgomery. The Human Parrot and Other Essays. Oxford, 1931.

Blackmur, R. P., "The Later Poetry of W. B. Yeats," in *Critiques and Essays in Criticism,* ed. by R. W. Stallman. New York, 1949.

Bodkin, Maud. Archetypal Patterns in Poetry. London, 1934.
Chaps. ii, iii, vi.

Bradley, A. C., "Poetry for Poetry's Sake," in *Oxford Lectures on Poetry.* London, 1950.

Brooks, Cleanth, "The Problem of Belief and the Problem of Cognition," in *The Well Wrought Urn*. New York, 1947.

Carnap, Rudolf. Philosophy and Logical Syntax. London, 1935. Chap i.

Crane, Ronald S. The Languages of Criticism and the Structure of Poetry. Toronto, 1953.

Croce, Benedetto. Aesthetics. New York, 1922. 2d ed.

Daiches, David. Poetry and the Modern World. Chicago, 1940.

—— A Study of Literature. Ithaca, N.Y., 1948. Chap. ix.

Eliot, T. S., "Dante," in *Selected Essays 1917–1932*. London, 1932.

—— "Literature, Science, and Dogma," *The Dial,* Vol. LXXXII (1927).

—— "Poetry and Propaganda," in *Literary Opinion in America,* ed. by Morton Dauwen Zabel. New York, 1951.

—— "Religion and Literature," in *Essays Ancient and Modern*. New York, 1936.

—— "The Social Function of Poetry," in *On Poetry and Poets*. London, 1957.

—— The Use of Poetry and the Use of Criticism. London, 1933.

Evans, William Vincent. Belief and Art. Chicago, 1939.

Fairchild, Hoxie Neale. Religious Trends in English Poetry. New York, 1957. Vol. IV, chap. xx.

Forster, E. M. Anonymity: An Enquiry. London, 1925.

Harap, Louis, "What is Poetic Truth?" *Journal of Philosophy,* Vol. XXX (1933).

Heller, Erich. The Disinherited Mind. Cambridge, 1952. Pages 99–140.

Hopper, Stanley R., ed., Spiritual Problems in Contemporary Literature. New York, 1952.

Hospers, John. Meaning and Truth in the Arts. Chapel Hill, N.C., 1946.

Isenberg, Arnold, "The Problem of Belief," *The Journal of Aesthetics and Art Criticism,* Vol. XIII (1955).

James, D. G. Scepticism and Poetry. London, 1937.

Jarrett-Kerr, Martin, c.r. Studies in Literature and Belief. London, 1954.

Keast, W. R., "The 'New Criticism' and *King Lear,*" in *Critics and Criticism Ancient and Modern,* ed. by R. S. Crane. Chicago, 1952.

Krieger, Murray. The New Apologists for Poetry. Minneapolis, 1956.

Leavis, F. R. The Great Tradition. London, 1948.

Leon, Philip, "Aesthetic Knowledge," in *The Problems of Aesthetics,* ed. by Eliseo Vivas and Murray Krieger. New York, 1953.

Lewis, C. Day. The Poet's Way of Knowledge. Cambridge, 1957.

Maritain, Jacques. Art and Scholasticism. New York, 1930.

Murry, J. Middleton, "Beauty is Truth," *Symposium,* Vol. I (1930).

Nott, Kathleen. The Emperor's Clothes. London, 1953.

Pottle, Frederick A. The Idiom of Poetry. Ithaca, N.Y., 1946. Chaps. vii–ix.

Ransom, John Crowe. The New Criticism. Norfolk, Conn., 1941.

—— The World's Body. New York, 1938. Pages 143–65.

Richards, I. A., "Belief," *Symposium,* Vol. I (1930).

—— "Between Truth and Truth," *Symposium,* II (1931).

—— Coleridge on Imagination. London, 1934. Chaps. vi, viii.

—— Practical Criticism. London, 1930. Chap. vii.

Richards, I. A. Principles of Literary Criticism. London, 1934. Chap. xxxv.

—— Science and Poetry. London, 1926.

—— Speculative Instruments. London, 1955. Chaps. iii, xiv.

Rodway, A. E., "The Verification of Poetic Meaning," Essays in Criticism, Vol. III (1953).

Roellinger, Francis X. Jr., "Two Theories of Poetry as Knowledge," Southern Review, Vol. VII (1942).

Rooney, William Joseph. The Problem of "Poetry and Belief" in Contemporary Criticism. Washington, D.C., 1949.

Santayana, George. Interpretations of Poetry and Religion. New York, 1957.

Schwartz, Delmore, "Poetry and Belief in Thomas Hardy," in Critiques and Essays in Criticism, ed. by Robert W. Stallman. New York, 1949.

Stallman, Robert W., ed. The Critic's Notebook. Minneapolis, 1950. Part VII.

Tate, Allen, "Literature as Knowledge" and "Three Types of Poetry," in On the Limits of Poetry. New York, 1948.

Trilling, Lionel, "The Meaning of a Literary Idea," in The Liberal Imagination. New York, 1951.

Vivas, Eliseo, "Literature and Knowledge," in Creation and Discovery. New York, 1955.

Vivas, Eliseo, and Murray Krieger, eds. The Problems of Aesthetics. New York, 1953.

Weitz, Morris, "Art, Language and Truth," in The Problems of Aesthetics, ed. by Eliseo Vivas and Murray Krieger. New York, 1953.

Wheelwright, Philip. The Burning Fountain. Bloomington, Ind.,
    1954. Chap. xiii.
——— "Poetry and Logic," *Symposium,* Vol. I (1930).
Wimsatt, W. K. Jr. The Verbal Icon. Lexington, Ky., 1954.
Winters, Yvor. In Defense of Reason. Denver, 1947.

Supervising Committee, the English Institute, 1957

The Program

September 3 through September 7, 1957

Conferences

I. PUBLISHERS AND THE READING PUBLIC
Directed by RICHARD D. ALTICK, *Ohio State University*

1. The Reader-Writer-Critic Triangle
WILLIAM CHARVAT, *Ohio State University*

2. A Modern Publisher Looks at the Public
ALFRED A. KNOPF

3. "My Squeamish Public": Some Problems of Victorian Magazine Publishers and Editors
OSCAR MAURER, *University of Texas*

4. Publishers and Sinners: the Augustan View
IAN P. WATT, *University of California, Berkeley*

II. LITERATURE AND BELIEF
Directed by CLEANTH BROOKS, *Yale University*

1. Belief and the Suspension of Disbelief
M. H. ABRAMS, *Cornell University*

2. Tradition and Experience
DOUGLAS BUSH, *Harvard University*

3. Voice as Summons for Belief
WALTER J. ONG, S.J., *St. Louis University*

4. The Implications of an Organic Theory of Poetry
CLEANTH BROOKS, *Yale University*

III. PROSE STYLE IN AMERICAN FICTION
Directed by CARVEL COLLINS, *Massachusetts Institute of Technology*

1. The Development of Style in Nineteenth-Century American Fiction
HAROLD C. MARTIN, *Harvard University*

2. Style and Point of View in the Major Works of Mark Twain
JOHN C. GERBER, *State University of Iowa*

3. The Style of Henry James
CHARLES R. CROW, *University of Pittsburgh*

4. The Style of William Faulkner
   CARVEL COLLINS, *Massachusetts Institute of Technology*

IV. WALLACE STEVENS
   Directed by SAMUEL FRENCH MORSE, *Trinity College, Hartford*
   1. The Graded Exercises of *Harmonium*
      JOHN J. ENCK, *University of Wisconsin*

   2. The World as Meditation
      LOUIS L. MARTZ, *Yale University*

   3. Some Relations between Poetry and Painting
      MICHEL BENAMOU, *University of Michigan*

   4. The Native Element
      SAMUEL FRENCH MORSE, *Trinity College, Hartford*

Evening Meeting, September 5
      Advance from Broadway
      NORRIS HOUGHTON, *Phoenix Theatre, New York*

Registrants, 1957

Kenneth T. Abrams, Cornell University; M. H. Abrams, Cornell University; Ruth M. Adams, University of Rochester; Gellert Spencer Alleman, Rutgers University; Hubert C. Alleman, Columbia University; Russell K. Alspach, United States Military Academy; Richard D. Altick, Ohio State University; G. L. Anderson, New York University; Mother Thomas Aquinas, College of New Rochelle; George Arms, University of New Mexico.

Sister Anne Barbara, Emmanuel College; Cesar Lombardi Barber, Amherst College; Richard Kenneth Barksdale, North Carolina College; Phyllis Bartlett, Queens College; David W. Becker, Miami University; Michel Jean Benamou, University of Michigan; Robert Mark Benbow, Colby College; Alice Rhodus Bensen, Eastern Michigan College; John Walter Bicknell, Drew University; Philip Bordinat, Miami University; Edwin T. Bowden, University of Texas; Hoyt Edwin Bowen, Pfeiffer College; Brother Clementian Francis Bowers, De La Salle College; Reverend John Dominic Boyd, Bellarmine College; Mary Campbell Brill, West Virginia Wesleyan College; Charles Vyner Brooke, Southern Illinois University; Cleanth Brooks, Yale University;

Benjamin Brower, Harvard University; Louise Stephens Brown, Columbia College; Nathaniel Hapgood Brown, Columbia University; Mrs. W. Bryher; Brother Fidelian Burke, De La Salle College; Sister M. Vincentia Burns, Albertus Magnus College; Raymond S. Burns, Villanova University; Katherine Burton, Wheaton College; Douglas Bush, Harvard University; Mrs. Kathleen Derrigan Byrne, Seton Hill College.

Herbert Cahoon, Pierpont Morgan Library; Grace J. Calder, Hunter College; William Charvat, Ohio State University; Hugh C. G. Chase; Sister Mary Chrysostom, College of Mount Saint Vincent; Donald Lemen Clark, Columbia University; Mother Madeleine Clary, College of New Rochelle; James L. Clifford, Columbia University; Carvel Collins, Massachusetts Institute of Technology; Ralph Waterbury Condee, Pennsylvania State University; Frederick William Conner, University of Florida; Francis X. Connolly, Fordham University; Roberta Douglas Cornelius, Randolph-Macon Woman's College; Alexander Cowie, Wesleyan University; George Armour Craig, Amherst College; Lucille Crighton, Gulf Park College; James H. Croushore, Mary Washington College; Charles R. Crow, University of Pittsburgh; Reverend John Vincent Curry, LeMoyne College; Frank Daniel Curtin, Saint Lawrence University; Sister Mary Cyrille, Rosary College.

Loren K. Davidson, Ohio University; Robert Gorham Davis, Smith College; Francis X. Degnen, Saint John's University; Robert M. Dell, Pace College; Charlotte D'Evelyn, Mount Holyoke College; Sister Rose Bernard Donna, College of Saint Rose; Daniel Donno, Queens College; Elizabeth Story Donno, Queens College; Agnes McNeill Donohue, Barat College; Lenthiel

Howell Downs, Denison University; Elizabeth Drew, Smith College; Owen Duston, Wabash College.

Edward R. Easton, Pace College; Ursula Elizabeth Eder, Vassar College; William Elton, University of California, Riverside; John Jacob Enck, University of Wisconsin; Martha W. England, Queens College; David V. Erdman, New York Public Library; Sister Mary Estelle, Albertus Magnus College; Robert Owen Evans, University of Kentucky.

Peter Francis Fisher, Royal Military College of Canada; Edward Garland Fletcher, University of Texas; Frank Cudworth Flint, Dartmouth College; Claude R. Flory, Florida State University; Elizabeth S. Foster, Oberlin College; Sister Mary Francis, College of Mount Saint Vincent; John Frederick Frank, Rider College; Northrop Frye, Victoria College, University of Toronto.

Giuseppi Galigani, University of Pisa; Geraldine Ann Gallagher, Shepherd College; Katherine H. Gatch, Hunter College; John C. Gerber, State University of Iowa; Carol Gesner, Berea College; Walker Gibson, Washington Square College, New York University; Ray Ginger, Alfred A. Knopf, Inc.; Leonard Goldstein, Rutgers University; Herbert I. Goldstone, New York State University Teachers College, Cortland; Douglas Grant, University College, University of Toronto; Helen Teresa Greany, Jersey City State Teachers College; Elizabeth Alden Green, Mount Holyoke College; Donald Johnson Greene; Richard Leighton Greene, Wesleyan University; William Wayne Griffith, Mary Washington College; Mrs. Hazel I. Guyol.

Gordon Sherman Haight, Yale University; Robert Halsband, Hunter College; Victor Michael Hamm, Marquette University; John Edward Hardy, University of Notre Dame; Katharine

Sumner Harris, Queens College; John A. Hart, Carnegie Institute of Technology; Miriam Margaret Heffernan, Brooklyn College; Eldon C. Hill, Miami University; William Bernard Hill; Frederick Whiley Hilles, Yale University; C. Fenno Hoffman, Jr., Middlebury College; John Hollander, Connecticut College; Helene Maxwell Hooker, Queens College; Andrew G. Hoover, Oberlin College; Vivian Constance Hopkins, New York State College for Teachers, Albany; Joyce Mary Horner, Mount Holyoke College; Norris Houghton, Phoenix Theatre; Donald R. Howard, Ohio State University; Muriel J. Hughes, University of Vermont; Dalma M. Hunyadi, Lewis College; Julia H. Hysham, Skidmore College.

William Alexander Jamison, Jr., University of Rochester; Eleanor Croysdale Jared, University of Western Ontario; Mackie Langham Jarrell, Connecticut College; Sears Reynolds Jayne, University of Virginia; S. F. Johnson, Columbia University; Sister Julie, Rosary College.

Louise Kannapell, Nazareth College; Ralph James Kaufmann, University of Rochester; Norman Kelvin, Rutgers University; John Pendy Kirby, Randolph-Macon Woman's College; Clara Marburg Kirk, Rutgers University; Rudolph Kirk, Rutgers University; Carl Frederick Klinck, University of Western Ontario; Mary Etta Knapp, Western College for Women; Miriam Hermanos Knapp, Columbia University; Alfred A. Knopf; Kathrine Koller, University of Rochester; Ervin James Korges, University of Alabama; Karl Kroeber, University of Wisconsin; Frank A. Krutzke, Colorado College.

Lincoln Filene Ladd, North Carolina State College; Reverend

John P. Lahey, Fordham University; Sidney Stevens Lamb, Sir George Williams College; Reverend Henry St. C. Lavin, Fordham University; Gaylord C. Leroy, Temple University; Harry Levin, Harvard University; Ellen Douglass Leyburn, Agnes Scott College; Leonard Lief, Hunter College; Dwight Newton Lindley, Hamilton College; Chun-Jo Liu, Vassar College; Louis G. Locke, Madison College; Barry William Long, New York University.

Sister Edwin Mary McBride, Webster College; Darryl McCall, University of Florida; Charles John McCann, Canisius College; John McChesney, Hotchkiss School; Sister Mary Immaculate McElroy, Saint Vincent Ferrer Convent; George Middleton McEwen, University of Michigan; George McFadden, Temple University; Richard S. McIntyre; Kenneth MacLean, Victoria College, University of Toronto; Millar MacLure, Victoria College, University of Toronto; Helen Neill McMaster, Sarah Lawrence College; Mother C. E. Maguire, Newton College of the Sacred Heart; Sister Elizabeth Marian, College of Mount Saint Vincent; Sister Julia Marie, College of Mount Saint Vincent; Kenneth B. Marshall, Denison University; Mary H. Marshall, Syracuse University; Thomas F. Marshall, Kent State University; Harold C. Martin, Harvard University; Louis Lohr Martz, Yale University; Dorothy Mateer, College of Wooster; Oscar Maurer, University of Texas; Richard McMath Mears, Catawba College; Paul L. Millane, McGraw-Hill Book Company; Stuart Miller, Oberlin College; Dorothy Siegfrieda Milton, Ferris Institute; Francis E. Mineka, Cornell University; Louie M. Miner; Sister Jeanne Pierre Mittnight, College of Saint Rose; Samuel French Morse, Trinity College.

George L. Nesbit, Hamilton College; John William Nichol, Denison University; Reverend William Thomas Noon, Canisius College; Elizabeth M. Nugent, Georgetown University.

Robert Matheson O'Clair, Harvard University; Reverend Joseph Eugene O'Neill, Fordham University; Reverend Walter J. Ong, Saint Louis University; James M. Osborn, Yale University.

Stephen Curtiss Paine, Salem College; Alice Parker, Lindenwood College; Sister Marie Paula, College of Mount Saint Vincent; Norman Holmes Pearson, Yale University; Harry William Pedicord; William W. Peery, Tulane University; Henry Popkin, Brandeis University; Lee Harris Potter, DePauw University; Abbie Findlay Potts, Rockford College; George Foster Provost, Duquesne University; Max Putzel, University of Connecticut.

Richard Edgecombe Quaintance, Jr., Yale University; Reverend Charles Joaquin Quirk, Loyola University of the South.

Isabel E. Rathborne, Hunter College; Charles Arthur Ray, North Carolina College; Libuse L. Reed, Ohio Wesleyan University; Sister Catherine Regina, College of Mount Saint Vincent; Keith Norton Richwine, West Virginia Wesleyan; Carmen L. Rivera, Mary Washington College; Francis X. Roellinger, Jr., Oberlin College; Rebecca Dorothy Ruggles, Brooklyn College; Donald Jacob Rulfs, North Carolina State College.

Irene Samuel, Hunter College; C. Earle Sanborn, University of Western Ontario; Joseph Schiffman, Long Island University; Bernard N. Schilling, University of Rochester; Sister Mary Thecla Schmidt, Seton Hill College; Helene B. M. Schnabel; Elisabeth Wintersteen Schneider, Temple University; Flora Rheta Schreiber, New School for Social Research; Aurelia Scott, Wagner College; Helen M. Scurr, University of Bridgeport; Frank Eugene Seward,

Catholic University of America; Richard Sexton, Fordham University School of Business; Norman Silverstein, Queens College; William Sloane, Dickinson College; Phyllis Patricia Smith, Mount Holyoke College; Stephen Sadler Stanton, University of Michigan; Jess M. Stein, Random House, Inc.; Erwin Ray Steinberg, Carnegie Institute of Technology; Helen L. Stevens, Illinois Institute of Technology; John H. Sutherland, Colby College; Barbara Swain, Vassar College; Paul Joseph Sweeney, Xavier University.

Anne Robb Taylor, Connecticut College; Bryce Thomas, Pace College; Doris Stevens Thompson, Russell Sage College; A. R. Towers, Queens College; Sister Marie of the Trinity, Emmanuel College; Carrington Cabell Tutwiler, Virginia Military Institute.

S. O. A. Ullmann, Union College.

Albert Douglass Van Nostrand, Brown University; Howard P. Vincent, Illinois Institute of Technology; Reverend Vianney Vormwald, Siena College; Richard Beckman Vowles, University of Florida.

Willis J. Wager, Boston University; Hyatt H. Waggoner, Brown University; Richard Long Waidelich, Goucher College; Eugene M. Waith, Yale University; Andrew Jackson Walker, Georgia Institute of Technology; Charlotte Crawford Watkins, Howard University; Robert Winthrop Watson, Women's College of the University of North Carolina; Ian Pierre Watt, University of California, Berkeley; Charles Henry Watts, II, Brown University; Allen Leaming Weatherby, Drew University; Minnie E. Wells, University of Alaska; John Calely Wentz, Rutgers University; Reverend Norman Weyand, Loyola University; Burton Maynard Wheeler, Washington University; Thomas R. Whitaker, Oberlin College; Mother Elizabeth White, Newton College of the Sacred Heart; J. Edwin Whitesell, University of South Carolina; Elkin Calhoun Wilson, New York University; Robert H. Wilson, Northern Illinois State College; William Kurtz Wimsatt, Jr., Yale University; Calhoun Winton, Dartmouth College; Philip M. Withim, Bucknell University; Marion Witt, Hunter College; Michael Jonas Wolff, Indiana University; Ross Greig Woodman, University of Western Ontario.

Joseph B. Yokelson, Colby College; James Dean Young, Georgia Institute of Technology.